Modern Critical Interpretations

# William Blake's
# The Marriage of Heaven and Hell

# Modern Critical Interpretations

*These and other titles in preparation*

Modern Critical Interpretations

William Blake's
# The Marriage of Heaven and Hell

*Edited and with an introduction by*

Harold Bloom
*Sterling Professor of the Humanities*
*Yale University*

*Chelsea House Publishers* ◊ *1987*

NEW YORK ◊ NEW HAVEN ◊ PHILADELPHIA

© 1987 by Chelsea House Publishers, a division of
Chelsea House Educational Communications, Inc.,
    95 Madison Avenue, New York, NY 10016
    345 Whitney Avenue, New Haven, CT 06511
    5014 West Chester Pike, Edgemont, PA 19028

Printed and bound in the United States of America

∞The paper used in this publication meets the minimum requirements
of the American National Standard for Permanence of Paper for Printed
Library Materials, Z39.48-1984.

Library of Congress Cataloging-in-Publication Data

William Blake's The Marriage of Heaven and Hell.

   (Modern critical interpretations)
   Bibliography: p.
   Includes index.
   1. Blake, William, 1757–1827. Marriage of Heaven
and Hell. I. Bloom, Harold. II. Series.
PR4144.M33W5 1987          821'.7          86-29872
ISBN 0-87754-729-7

# Contents

# Editor's Note

This book gathers together what I judge to be the most useful criticism available on William Blake's *The Marriage of Heaven and Hell,* an "illuminated book" that proclaims the poet-engraver's maturation into a prophet, a social revolutionary, and an apocalyptic satirist whose only rival in the language is the Jonathan Swift of *A Tale of the Tub.* The critical essays here are reprinted in the chronological order of their original publication. I am grateful to Hillary Kelleher for her aid in editing this volume.

My introduction, written in 1962 as part of a study of Blake, attempts a full reading of the *Marriage* as the central formulation of what I take to be Blake's apocalyptic humanism. Northrop Frye's beautiful remarks on the visionary argument of the *Marriage* from his superb *Fearful Symmetry* begin the chronological sequence, which continues with David V. Erdman's pathbreaking analysis of the engraved book's precise relation to the revolutionary politics of Blake's age. My own early account of the dialectic of the *Marriage* follows, and is the prelude to Thomas R. Frosch's important investigation, from a Freudian perspective, of Blake and the body, emphasizing how crucially Blake meant his hopes for our coming to possess enlarged and more numerous senses than we labor with in our fallen cosmos.

In Martin K. Nurmi's exegesis of the Blakean distinction between contraries and negations, an attempt is made to establish Blake's ontological sense of our "polar being." More radically, Leopold Damrosch examines the problem of dualism in the *Marriage,* and concludes that Blake settles for different *kinds* of contraries, since the concept of contraries proves not comprehensive enough to organize the whole of Blake's thought.

Diane Hume George, the most responsible and learned of Blake's feminist scholar-critics, usefully contrasts the perspectives of the *Marriage* and of Freud. The social context of the *Marriage,* first explored by Erdman, is further developed by Stewart Crehan, partly in terms of economic theories contemporary with Blake.

In this book's final essay, Robert F. Gleckner locates the *Marriage* in relation to Blake's prime precursors as poets of visionary epic, Spenser and Milton. Gleckner's critique of all prior modes of reading the *Marriage,* my own included, returns us full circle to the introduction, and to my lifelong conviction that *The Marriage of Heaven and Hell* is one of those rare works that can compel crucial and salutary spiritual, psychological, and intellectual changes in a sensitive and informed reader.

# Introduction

About 1788, Blake read and annotated Swedenborg's *Wisdom of Angels Concerning Divine Love and Divine Wisdom*. Blake was not brought up a Swedenborgian, that being one of the many biographical myths about him that David Erdman has demonstrated to be inaccurate or irrelevant. Much in Swedenborg must have seemed unimaginative to Blake from the start, but clearly Blake progressed from feeling some affinity with Swedenborg to a strong sense of outrage, as he realized how limited the affinity actually was. Blake read as he lived, painted, and wrote: to correct other men's visions, not into Blake's own, but into forms that emphasized the autonomy of each human imagination, both as against "nature" or what our eyes see when they are tired and deathly, and as against any received notions that might seek to set limits to perception. So, to Swedenborg's "In all the Heavens there is no other Idea of God than that of a Man," Blake added:

> Man can have no idea of any thing greater than Man, as a cup cannot contain more than its capaciousness. But God is a man, not because he is so perciev'd by man, but because he is the creator of man.

Swedenborg touches upon a religious humanism, but halts his imagination before realizing its potential. Blake, as an artist, knows that his own best being is in his creations. So God, whose best creation is man, must find *his* own best being in man. Man is the form that God creates and loves, and so God must be a man. That the converse is not always true, that man is only partly God, is the burden that Blake's poems exist to lighten, and hope at last to annihilate.

Swedenborg, though he ended as a visionary and the founder of yet another Christian sect, had begun as a reasoner from nature, and his reports of what he took to be the spiritual world read now like parodies of the eighteenth-century search for a science of sciences. The result is that the direct satirical basis of much

From *Blake's Apocalypse: A Study in Poetic Argument.* © 1963 by Harold Bloom. Cornell University Press, 1970.

in *The Marriage of Heaven and Hell* has lost its point. Even if Swedenborg had any relevance to our condition now, we would not need Blake to satirize him. But Blake has much in common with Swift as a satirist. The satire in each has survived its victims, because the structure of that satire comprehends eternal types of intellectual error and spiritual self-deception. A reader of *The Marriage of Heaven and Hell* needs to know of Swedenborg only what Blake took him to be:

> O Swedenborg! strongest of men, the Samson
> shorn by the Churches,
> Shewing the Transgressors in Hell, the proud
> Warriors in Heaven,
> Heaven as a Punisher, & Hell as one under
> Punishment.
>
> *(Milton, 22:50–52)*

> He [Swedenborg] shews the folly of churches, & exposes hypocrites, till he imagines that all are religious, & himself the single one on earth that ever broke a net.
>
> *(The Marriage, 21)*

Swedenborg is the eternal type of the prophet who becomes a new kind of priest, and by becoming a church loses his imaginative strength, until he concludes by renewing the religious categories of judgment he came to expose as impostures. The psychological root of this ironic cycle of transformation is in the prophet's growing and pernicious conviction of his absolute uniqueness. The contempt of Blake for this kind of self-deception is based on a conviction that the entire process is another triumph of nature over the integrity of vision. Whatever faults of passion Blake possessed, and he recognized each of them in turn as they became relevant to his poetry, he never allowed himself to believe he was "the single one on earth that ever broke a net" of religious orthodoxy.

The literary form of Blake's *Marriage* is best named by Northrop Frye's term, an *anatomy,* or more traditionally a Menippean satire, characterized by its concern with intellectual error, its extraordinary diversity of subject-matter, a mixed verse-and-prose form, and a certain reliance on a symposium setting. Relentless experimenter as he was, Blake created in the *Marriage* what may even have surprised himself, so original is the work in its structure. It opens with a free-verse "Argument," and then passes to a statement of creative oppositions that Blake calls "Contraries." Two sets of contraries are then stated in a passage headed "The voice of the Devil," which concludes by a remarkable brief reading of Milton's *Paradise Lost.* Following is the first of five "Memorable Fancies," clearly originating as parodies of Swedenborg's "Memorable Relations," in which the Swedish visionary had described the wonders of the spiritual world. The first Memorable Fancy leads to the famous "Proverbs of Hell," seventy aphorisms unmatched in literature for their intellectual shock value. The remainder of the *Marriage* alternates Memorable Fancies with groupings of apocalyptic reflections. The first of these gives a brief history of religion; the next relates Blake's art to the "improvement of sensual enjoyment" that will precede the Apocalypse; and the final two deal with the strife of contraries again, and with the errors of Swedenborg. After the final Memorable Fancy, the whole work ends with a proverb previously gasped out in Tiriel's death agony: "One Law for the Lion & Ox is Oppression."

The unity of this structure is a dialectical one, and depends upon a progression in understanding, as one proceeds from engraved plate to engraved plate of the work. The title plate shows a sexual embrace amid flames, in its lower half; the upper part depicts wanderers between twisted trees, and a loss of Innocence beneath two trees of Mystery, with a raven overhead. The center of the plate features lovers rising upward from the flames, but aspiring towards the roots of the sinister trees above. The visual process is purely ironic; to rise *away* from the sexual fire can only lead to loss. This picture epitomizes the rhetorical emphasis of the *Marriage,* with its "diabolical" preference for desire over restraint, energy over reason. But the *sequence* of plates transcends this antinomian rhetoric, and demonstrates the necessity for both sets of creative oppositions. The Argument states the problem of the work's genesis: the breakthrough of the contraries into history. The Memorable Fancies are all on the rhetorical side of the "Devil," though they continually qualify the supposed demonism of that party. The sections between the Fancies carry forward the dialectic of the work; they exist to clarify the role of the contraries. Blake asks of his reader a subtle alternation of moods; to move constantly from a defiant celebration of hertofore repressed energies to a realization that the freed energies must accept a bounding outline, a lessened but still existent world of confining mental forms.

Our actual reading of *The Marriage of Heaven and Hell* can begin with a consideration of the title itself. Annotating Swedenborg's *Wisdom of Angels Concerning Divine Love and Divine Wisdom* in 1788, Blake came to a particular statement urgently needing ironic correction by a restatement ostensibly in agreement with it:

> SWEDENBORG: Man is only a Recipient of Life. From this Cause it is, that Man, from his own hereditary Evil, reacts against God; but so far as he believes that all his Life is from God, and every Good of Life from the Action of God, and every Evil of Life from the reaction of Man, Reaction thus becomes correspondent with Action, and Man acts with God as from himself.

BLAKE: Good & Evil are here both Good & the two contraries
Married.

It is probable that this interchange is the seed of *The Marriage of Heaven
and Hell.* Blake perceives in Swedenborg an instance of the two moral contraries
of good and evil being so held in relation to each other that they exist in harmony without losing their individual characteristics. The key term in the Swedenborg passage is "correspondent"; in the Blake comment it is "contraries." In
Swedenborg, "correspondent" means that the Reaction and Action of the passage
do subsume one another; they become for pragmatic purposes a unity of mutual
absorption. But Blake's "contraries" never absorb one another; and his point is
that the "Good & Evil" of Swedenborg were never really moral good and moral
evil, but merely forms of the good in the first place. For Blake's Man creates life,
and does not only receive it from God. All contraries are born within the human
existence: Blake's last note on Swedenborg's *Divine Love* is: "Heaven & Hell are
born together." Yet Swedenborg either forgot or had never learned this. Reading
Swedenborg's *Divine Providence* two years later, in 1790, Blake is outraged at
the flowering of Swedenborg's error into the dead fruit of the doctrine of
Predestination. From this outrage the title of Blake's *Marriage* takes its origin.

Blake's title also has ironic reference to Swedenborg's *Heaven and Hell and
their Wonders,* though his annotated copy of that book is lost. So is his copy
of Swedenborg on the *Last Judgment,* where it was declared that:

> The evil are cast into the hells, and the good elevated into heaven,
> and thus that all things are reduced into order, the spiritual equilibrium
> between good and evil, or between heaven and hell, being thence
> restored. . . . This Last Judgment was commenced in the beginning
> of the year 1757.

That was the year of Blake's birth, and so Swedenborg's heaven and Blake's
hell were born together. In 1790, Blake was thirty-three years old, and thirty-
three years had elapsed since the Last Judgment in the spiritual world. The outward apocalypse had been slow in coming, but by 1790 it must have seemed
to Blake that the prophesied time-of-troubles that must precede apocalypse was
surely at hand. We have seen Blake tracing those portents in his poem *The French
Revolution.* Though the satiric motive for the *Marriage* is Blake's desire to expose
Swedenborg, the work has a half-serious religious and political impulse within
it as well. The French Revolution and the British reaction to it suggest to Blake
a contemporary manifestation of the ancient turning over of a prophetic cycle.
The *Marriage's* Argument begins:

> Rintrah roars & shakes his fires in the
> burden'd air;

Hungry clouds swag on the deep.

As with the appearance of Luvah in *The Book of Thel,* and Urizen in *Visions of the Daughters of Albion,* here we encounter another introduction of a symbolic personage before Blake is quite ready to make full use of him. What this suggests is that Blake may have formulated a large part of his mythology some years before he incorporated it into his poetry. Rintrah is Blake's Angry Man, a John the Baptist or Elijah figure, the wrathful spirit of prophecy driven out into the wilderness. The outcry and fires of Rintrah are in the burdened clouds, hungry with portents, that heavily sink down on the deep that separates France from England. The cycle of human existence turns over, and the just man is driven out by the villain:

> Once meek, and in a perilous path,
> The just man kept his course along
> The vale of death.
> Roses are planted where thorns grow,
> And on the barren heath
> Sing the honey bees.
>
> Then the perilous path was planted,
> And a river and a spring
> On every cliff and tomb,
> And on the bleached bones
> Red clay brought forth;
>
> Till the villain left the paths of ease,
> To walk in perilous paths, and drive
> The just man into barren climes.
>
> Now the sneaking serpent walks
> In mild humility,
> And the just man rages in the wilds
> Where lions roam.

The meek just man begins by regulating his course in that perilous path of life that always is shadowed by death. Yet that path is already involved in existential contraries; roses and thorns come up together, and the honey bees sing on a heath with no provision for them. The joy and grief of this existence are woven too fine; the course kept by the just man is *planted,* and becomes a natural custom, or falls into vegetative existence. Yet this naturalizing of the just man is a creation as well as a fall. The barrenness of cliff and tomb yields to a water that people may drink, and on the bleached bones of an earlier world the red clay that is Adam is brough forth.

But a turning natural cycle is an invitation for the villain, who leaves the paths of ease (which must be in a realm of non-existence, since for Blake existence is a struggle) and usurps the just man's place. Very likely on the social level this is a parable of exploitation. The villain becomes the sneaking serpent or "Angel" of mild humility, who stalks through the now ironically titled "perilous paths," and the just man becomes the "Devil" or outcast prophet, menaced by everything in nature that fears prophecy. The contraries of natural cycle are not true contraries, else the cycle could not go on unchanged. So Blake breaks off his "Argument" and begins to state the laws of progression:

> As a new heaven is begun, and it is now thirty-three years since its advent: the Eternal Hell revives. And lo! Swedenborg is the Angel sitting at the tomb: his writings are the linen clothes folded up. Now is the dominion of Edom, & the return of Adam into Paradise. See Isaiah XXXIV & XXXV Chap.

Blake is thirty-three, and remembers that Christ rose in the body at that age. Swedenborg sits at the tomb, Angel to Blake's Devil, to testify that Blake has awakened from the error of death into the more abundant life of the risen body. Poor Swedenborg's writings are but the linen clothes folded up, neatly put aside by Blake, who does not need the coverings of death to shield his passionate body from apocalyptic light. For the prophesied times are come; the dominion of Edom is at hand. The blessing of Esau, the red man of Edom, was that he should some day have dominion over Jacob. The prophet Isaiah saw this red man coming from Edom, with the day of vengeance in his heart, and knew this to be the troubled time before the Judgment, when Adam would at last return into Paradise. In 1790 Edom is France, and the red man will soon be identified as Blake's Orc, Spirit of Revolt, who seems a creature from Hell to those dwelling at ease in the Jacob or Israel that is Pitt's England.

The red man comes into Isaiah's vision late, at the start of chapter 63, where the judging climax begins to gather together. Blake's own reference is earlier; to two contrary chapters, 34 and 35, for some historical progression will be necessary before England attains to its climax. In chapter 34 the indignation of the Lord is upon all nations, and the wild beasts of the desert come to possess the world. But in chapter 35 the troubles yield to revelation: the eyes of the blind are opened, waters break out in the wilderness, and the perilous path becomes the highway of holiness upon which the redeemed shall walk. Both states, the outcast and the redeemed, are crucial; to us and to one another. For:

> Without Contraries is no progression. Attraction and Repulsion, Reason and Energy, Love and Hate, are necessary to Human existence.
> From these contraries spring what the religious call Good & Evil.

Good is the passive that obeys Reason. Evil is the active springing
from Energy.
Good is Heaven. Evil is Hell.

The philosopher Heraclitus condemned Homer for praying that strife might
perish from among gods and men, and said that the poet did not see that he
was praying for the destruction of the universe. The vision of Heraclitus is of
an attunement of opposite tensions, of mortals and immortals living the others'
death and dying the others' life. Blake read little with any care besides the Bible
and Milton; he is not likely to have derived anything really central to him from
ancient philosophy, or from the theosophy of the Cabala or Boehme. His doctrine or image of contraries is his own, and the analogues in Heraclitus or in
Blake's own contemporary, Hegel, are chiefly interesting as contrasts. For
Heraclitus, Good and Evil were one; for Blake they were not the inseparable
halves of the same thing, but merely born together, as Milton had believed. For
Hegel, opposites were raised to a higher power when they were transcended
by synthesis; for Blake, opposites remained creative only so long as each remained
immanent. Good and Evil could not refute one another, for each was only what
the religious called Good and Evil, passive and active, restrained and unrestrained.

The usual misinterpretation of Blake's contraries (stemming from Swinburne)
is that they represent a simple inversion of orthodox moral categories. Blake
is then pictured like Milton's Satan on Mount Niphates, passionately declaim-
ing: "Evil be thou my Good." Blake of course is doing nothing of the kind;
he is denying the orthodox categories altogether, and opposing himself both to
moral "good" and moral "evil." Frye usefully remarks that the Swinburnean
error in interpretation "ignores the fact that Blake attaches two meanings to
the word 'hell,' one real and the other ironic." The real hell is in the fearful
obsessions of the Selfhood; the ironic one is that just quoted from the *Marriage*:
an upsurge of desire whose energetic appearance frightens the Selfhood into the
conviction that such intensity must stem from an external hell.

From this point on, the vocabulary of the *Marriage* is altogether ironic, and
requires close attention. If Hell is the active springing from Energy, and the
Eternal Hell revives with Blake's assumption of the Christological role, then "The
voice of the Devil" that follows is Blake's own, but diabolical only because it
will seem so to Swedenborg or any other priestly Angel. The Devil's voice attacks the dualism of Christian tradition, the negation of setting the body's energy
as evil against the soul's reason as good. Against these "Errors" the Devil Blake
sets his contraries:

1. Man has no Body distinct from his Soul; for that call'd Body
is a portion of Soul discern'd by the five Senses, the chief inlets of
Soul in this age.

2. Energy is the only life, and is from the Body; and Reason is the bound or outward circumference of Energy.

3. Energy is Eternal Delight.

Blake is not saying that the soul is part of the body, but that the body is the outward circumference or boundary of the soul. In former ages, Blake implies, the more numerous and enlarged senses of man were able to discern a larger portion of the soul than the five senses can now. But what *can* be discerned of the soul now is chiefly the body; if the body is inadequate, it is nevertheless by necessity the way back to the soul. Asceticism is then exactly the wrong way to handle the body. It is by an increase and not a diminishment of sensual enjoyment that we can begin to expand our souls to their former dimensions. Donne in *The Extasie* affirms that the soul must repair first to the body before it can flow into another soul, but Donne's language is paradoxical and his remarkable poem abides in a philosophical dualism. But Blake really does believe that Energy is the only life, and is from the body, so that the greater wealth of a more abundant life, a more capable soul, must be the body's gift. The body's exuberance is the eternal delight that Coleridge and Wordsworth were to identify as the joy that alone made possible any artistic creation. For Blake, the running-down of that delight defines the place of reason in the creative life; the outward circumference where a vision recedes into merely natural light. In an ironic play upon an ancient Christian adage, the mind of the archetypal creator is for Blake an everlasting circle whose exuberant center is everywhere, and whose reasonable circumference is nowhere.

The archetypal creation, for Blake, was not the outward nature of the Coleridgean Primary Imagination, but the complete vision exuberantly manifested in the King James Bible. If a single poet since the Prophets and Jesus had incarnated that archetypal creative mind for Blake, surely that poet could only be John Milton. The *Marriage* passes therefore to the failure (as Blake saw it) of final exuberance in the maker of *Paradise Lost*. Plates 5 and 6 are a reading of the great English epic deliberately, which is to say ironically, from a Devil's point of view. Why did Milton restrain his poet's desire, and how did the restrainer, or reason, usurp desire's place and come to govern the unwilling poet?

> Those who restrain desire, do so because theirs is weak enough to be restrained; and the restrainer or reason usurps its place & governs the unwilling.
> And being restrain'd, it by degrees becomes passive, till it is only the shadow of desire.
> The history of this is written in Paradise Lost, & the Governor or Reason is call'd Messiah.
> And the original Archangel, or possessor of the command of the

heavenly host, is call'd the Devil or Satan, and his children are call'd Sin and Death.

But in the Book of Job, Milton's Messiah is call'd Satan.

For this history has been adopted by both parties.

It indeed appear'd to Reason as if Desire was cast out; but the Devil's account is, that the Messiah fell, & formed a heaven of what he stole from the Abyss.

This is shewn in the Gospel, where he prays to the Father to send the comforter, or Desire that Reason may have Ideas to build on; the Jehovah of the Bible being no other than he who dwells in flaming fire.

Know that after Christ's death, he became Jehovah.

But in Milton, the Father is Destiny, the Son a Ratio of the five senses, & the Holy-ghost, Vacuum!

*Note.* The reason Milton wrote in fetters when he wrote of Angels & God, and at liberty when of Devils & Hell, is because he was a true Poet and of the Devil's party without knowing it.

Few passages of literary analysis, and this is surpassingly excellent analysis, have been as misread as Blake's excursus on *Paradise Lost.* The traditional misinterpretation, with its distinguished lineage from Swinburne to C. S. Lewis, holds that Blake's reading is an antinomian one. But Blake is as uninterested in moral evil as he is in moral good; neither category seems imaginative to him. *Paradise Lost* and the Book of Job are theodicies; they seek to justify the existence of moral evil by asserting the ultimate reality and providence of moral good. Against such theodicies, with their final appeal to the necessity of fallen nature, Blake makes a double attack, on the one hand rhetorical and ironic, on the other argumentative and prophetically serious. The rhetorical attack *seems* antinomian, but is actually aesthetic, and concerns the relative failure (in Blake's view) of both *Paradise Lost* and Job. The prophetic attack is as serious as Blake can make it, and seeks to correct Milton's error in vision.

*Paradise Lost,* Blake judges, is written out of Milton's despair of his earlier apocalyptic hopes, and is a Song of Experience, a poem that accepts the fallen world's restraint of human desire. Milton is willing to restrain the desires of Satan and Eve, or see them punished for not accepting such restraints, because his own desires for knowledge and for the complete fulfillment of his imaginative potential have become weak enough to be restrained. Reasoning from nature usurps the place of imaginative desire and governs Milton's visionary powers, though they are unwilling to be so governed. By degrees, Milton's exuberance of invention becomes passive, until it is only the shadow of the power that creates the opening books of *Paradise Lost* and the past prophetic glory of *Areopagitica.*

The inner history of this psychic process of repression is written in *Paradise Lost*, where it is externalized as the progressive inhibition of Satan, who is degraded by his fall, from active rebellion into passive plotting against the restraints of Right Reason. The restrainer, called Messiah by Milton, is called Satan in the Book of Job. Here Blake is at his most subtle. Milton's Messiah drives Satan out of Heaven with fire, and "Eternal wrath / Burnt after them to the bottomless pit." Hell is thus created by an act of Messiah. In the Book of Job a hell of external torment is created for Job by Satan, who serves as God's Accuser of sins, going to and fro in the earth to impute sin to the righteous.

This crucial resemblance between Milton's Christ and Job's Satan—that each creates a world of punishment, a categorical judgment that militates against mutual forgiveness of every vice—inspires Blake's blandest irony: "For this history has been adopted by both parties." The two parties are Devils—or true poets who write to correct orthodoxy, and Angels—or ruined poets and theologians who write to uphold moral and religious conventions. According to Blake, Milton was like Swedenborg in that he aged from a Devil into an Angel. It indeed appeared to Milton the theologian, that Satan or Desire was cast out into Hell, but the true poet or Devil, working away *within* Milton and the authors of the Bible, gave another account—though to read that account now we need to read Milton and the Bible in their "diabolical" sense.

This infernal sense of meaning is to Blake *the* poetic sense of Milton or Job or the Gospels. If it appeared to the curbers of desire that all illicit energies had been cast out into an abyss of heat without light, it appears to the supposed outcasts that the heaven of restraint, abandoned behind them, is only a stolen and frozen form, out of the many living forms constantly being created in the "abyss" of realized desires. The heaven of orthodoxy, or idea of restraint, was formed by the Messiah or Reason, but to get the stuff of creativity he had to "fall" into the energetic world of imaginings, or else Reason could have no ideas to build on. So the Gospel promise to send the comforter is a desire for Desire, and the answering Jehovah of imagination, the Jehovah of the Bible, is a creator who dwells in flaming fire, not in the cold light of Milton's static heaven. If the Son was truly human desire, and the Father, Desire removed from all encumbrances, then their identity in the resurrection of the human body is an identity of fire, of an impeded desire flaming into that which delights in its own form. But in Milton, the Father is not the self-determining form of fire, but the determined form of Destiny. The Son is not the human desire to attain a more imaginative body, but a Ratio of the five senses, a reductive argument from the limitations of natural perception. And the comforter or Holy Ghost is not a mediating desire binding man to his envisioned fulfillment, but rather a vacuum, for he is not there at all, in a poem that places all positive action in the past, and assigns to its historical present a choice only of obedient passivity or demonic defiance. Yet, as Blake's altogether ironic *Note* to this section adds, Milton the poet could not be content with this desperate quietism. Energy and desire enter into the poem when Milton writes at liberty, for Milton's greatness was, at last, in spite of himself. Because he was a true poet, his creative exuberance burst the fetters of Right Reason, and the Satan who dominates the first third of the poem came into his powerful existence.

As a reading of *Paradise Lost,* there is much to be said against this, and more to be said for it than most contemporary critics of Milton would now acknowledge. But whether Blake's reading of Milton is correct is not altogether relevant to a reader's understanding of the *Marriage.* What matters is that momentarily he learn to read the poem as Blake read it.

When Milton's Satan goes off on his perilous journey through chaos to the earth in book 2 of *Paradise Lost,* his fallen host remains behind him in Hell, where they busy themselves with their equivalents of Olympian games, with composing and singing poems on their fate, with metaphysical and ethical discussions, and with explorations of their sad new world. One need not endorse Milton's theology to feel the force of his point: detached from God, such activities are demonic, and these enjoyments of fallen genius are sterile because they seek to serve as their own ends. But Blake's next section, the first of his Memorable Fancies, is an apt reply to Milton. Blake goes "walking among the fires of hell, delighted with the enjoyments of genius, which to Angels look like torment and insanity." To walk among those fires is to compose a poem or engrave a picture, and to collect the Proverbs of Hell, as Blake proceeds to do, is to express the laws of artistic creation in a series of aphorisms. When Blake came home from his proverb-collecting:

> On the abyss of the five senses, where a flat sided steep frowns over
> the present world, I saw a mighty Devil folded in black clouds, hover-
> ing on the sides of the rock: with corroding fires he wrote the follow-
> ing sentence now perceived by the minds of men, and read by them
> on earth:

> > How do you know but ev'ry Bird that cuts
> > the airy way,
> > Is an immense world of delight, clos'd by
> > your senses five?

The Devil is the artist William Blake, at work engraving the *Marriage,* and the corroding fires refer metaphorically both to his engraving technique and the satiric function of the *Marriage.* The flat-sided steep, frowning over the present world, is fallen human consciousness, and Blake is an old Rocky Face like the Yeats of *The Gyres* whom he influenced. The stony cavern of the mind has been broken open by Blake's art; the imagination rises from the mind's abyss and seeks more expanded senses than the five making up that abyss. The gnomic couplet etched by the Devil Blake is adapted from one of Thomas Chatterton's best poems, and is meant to serve as an introductory motto to the following Proverbs of Hell. In thus using Chatterton, Blake precedes Keats in honoring that Rimbaud of the English eighteenth century as a prophet of later poets' sensibilities.

Chatterton, for Blake, knew in his life, if not altogether in his work, that every object of natural perception contained an immense world of delight, closed off from us by the inadequacy of our five senses as we tended to use them in our minimal perceptions. The idea of raising our intensity of perception and so triumphing over nature *through nature* is the central idea of the Proverbs of Hell. Sexual exuberance, breaking the bounds of restraint and entering a fullness that Angelic Reason considers excess, will lead to a perception of a redeemed nature, though this perception itself must seem unlawful to fallen reason. The Proverbs emphasize an antinomian rhetoric but expect the reader to recognize the implicit argument that underlies and finally absorbs this fierce vocabulary. Blake is not saying that active evil is morally better than passive good, though he wants the shock value that such a statement would have. Blake's good is the active springing from energy; there is therefore no such thing as a passive good, except to the Angels who identify act and evil. Blake's definition of an act is only implied in the *Marriage*, but had been set down clearly by him in 1788 when he annotated the aphorisms of his contemporary, the Swiss poet and theologian Johann Kaspar Lavater:

> There is a strong objection to Lavater's principles (as I understand them) & that is He makes every thing originate in its accident; he makes the vicious propensity not only a leading feature of the man, but the stamina on which all his virtues grow. But as I understand Vice it is a Negative. It does not signify what the laws of Kings & Priests have call'd Vice; we who are philosophers ought not to call the Staminal Virtues of Humanity by the same name that we call the omissions of intellect springing from poverty.
>
> Every man's leading propensity ought to be call'd his leading Virtue & his good Angel. But the Philosophy of Causes & Consequences misled Lavater as it has all his Cotemporaries. Each thing is its own cause & its own effect. Accident is the omission of act in self & the hindering of act in another; This is Vice, but all Act [from Individual propensity] is Virtue. To hinder another is not an act; it is the contrary; it is a restraint on action both in ourselves & in the person

hinder'd, for he who hinders another omits his own duty at the same time.

Murder is Hindering Another.

Theft is Hindering Another.

Backbiting, Undermining, Circumventing, & whatever is Negative is Vice. But the origin of this mistake in Lavater & his cotemporaries is, They suppose that Woman's Love is Sin; in consequence all the Loves & Graces with them are Sin.

Of all Blake's annotations upon other writers, this seems to me the most profound, and the most central for a reader's understanding of Blake himself. Here indeed is the imaginative seed of not only the Proverbs of Hell but the whole of the *Marriage,* and of Blake's ideas of good and evil to the end of his life. What is hindrance and not action is evil, whether one hinders the self or another. Restraint for Blake is a mode of indecision, and proceeds from a mind in chaos. Decision, true act, proceeds from the whole man, the imaginative mind, and must be good, for whatever is negative is a restraint upon another, and not an act. Act stems from the only wealth, from life, but restraint is an omission of intellect, and springs from the poverty of lifelessness, the absence of the exuberance of mind delighting in its own forming powers. The paradoxes of Blake's Proverbs of Hell nearly always arise from an ironic awareness of the gap between "what the laws of Kings & Priests have call'd Vice" and what an artist sees as Vice: "the omission of act in self & the hindering of act in another."

In form, Blake's Proverbs parody what he might have called the "Proverbs of Heaven," the Book of Proverbs in the Hebrew Bible, which claim "to give subtility to the simple, to the young man knowledge and discretion." In contrast, Blake's Proverbs exist to break down orthodox categories of thought and morality. To accomplish this end Blake employs an apparent dissociation of customary meanings, both within many of the Proverbs and in their curious disarrangement. Since the Proverbs seek to destroy a pattern of preconceived responses, they rely on a final association of meanings after the initial dissociation has done its work.

The reader can arrive at this association by considering the Proverbs as falling into four overlapping groups, largely defined by their imagery. The first is clearly and intensely sexual, so intense that in it the act of sexual union assumes the mythic dimension familiar to us from the work of D. H. Lawrence. In the Proverbs, this sexual imagery is presented in a variety of ironic disguises, including the sacraments of baptism and communion, with their water and wine symbolism, and a complex association of plowing and harvest imagery with the idea of the fulfillment of prayer. Thus, "In seed time learn, in harvest teach, in winter enjoy" looks like a traditional description of man's life, but refers also to the sexual rites of initiation. To "Drive your cart and plow over the bones of the dead" is to renew human life by a refreshment of sexuality, even at the cost of defying the codes of the past. In the third Proverb, "The road of excess leads to the palace of wisdom," a second grouping of ideas and images are introduced. To increase sexual fulfillment is to take what the Angels consider the road of excess that will lead one to the palace of the diabolical principle. But this excess Blake considers as the contrary to the deliberate self-frustration of the Angels, expressed in the next Proverb, which is a brilliant allegorical story in one sentence: "Prudence is a rich, ugly old maid courted by Incapacity." Repressed energy culminates in neurosis: "He who desires but acts not, breeds pestilence." But what is genuinely acted upon may be injured yet is augmented: "The cut worm forgives the plow," an unequivocal image of phallic plenitude.

The themes of sexuality and excess meet in "Dip him in the river who loves water," for this cleansing baptism is the total immersion of the soul in the body's sexual wealth. Sexual excess as initiator meets its apocalyptic result in the following Proverbs, as the two further imagistic groupings, turning upon antinomianism and increased perceptiveness, make initial appearances. "A fool sees not the same tree that a wise man sees," for the wise man, as a creative Devil, sees the tree in a context more exuberant than any an unvitalized nature could sustain. The fool is self-condemned to a status of minimum vitality in nature, for "He whose face gives no light, shall never become a star." We see the light we emanate, and our creativeness is responsible not only for a different tree than the fool sees, but a different time in which vision takes place, for "Eternity is in love with the productions of time," not with time's passivities. In creation the oppressiveness of clock time vanishes, for "The busy bee has no time for sorrow" and "The hours of folly are measur'd by the clock; but of wisdom, no clock can measure."

In creative or human time, the restraints of fallen experience, the nets and traps of natural morality, tend to lose their immediacy, and desire and gratification are near-allied, an intimation of psychic health because "All wholesome food is caught without a net or a trap." The psychic abundance of the creative life scorns the conventionalizing forms of tradition, whether in the social elaborations of manners or the closed couplet of Augustan poetic decorum, for restricted forms ration the meager, not the prolific: "Bring out number, weight & measure in a year of dearth." The net of convention is broken by the imagination capable in itself, and in the consciousness of its own powers: "No bird soars too high, if he soars with his own wings." As for the offended conventions, they can do no harm, for "A dead body revenges not injuries."

So far the Proverbs of Hell have mostly been assaults upon conventional evasions of human energies. But Blake is not content to attack timidity; he desires also to replace the tired mind's naturalizations of its own best moments, by showing that mind the meaning of its own rejected strengths. In the human confrontation of another human, in the moment where the self acknowledges the full reality of another self, the relationship of equal immediacies is a recognition of the imaginative act itself: "The most sublime act is to set another before you."

We have considered, so far, the first seventeen of the seventy Proverbs of Hell. To go through each of the Proverbs in this way would be to usurp the reader's individuality of response, for the Proverbs should mean a variety of things, quite correctly, to different readers. There is perhaps more potential value in exploring the general pattern of the remaining Proverbs. The sexual and harvest images lead to the vision of excess, by which apparent foolishness culminates in the wisdom of a further horizon of human aspiration. This aspiration is emphasized obliquely in the group of antinomian Proverbs that concern animal powers and violently revenge stifled energies upon the restraints of Law and Religion. Hence: "The wrath of the lion is the wisdom of God," and "The tygers of wrath are wiser than the horses of instruction."

When this antinomian intensity is carried over into a human admonition, the result is deliberately shocking: "Sooner murder an infant in its cradle than nurse unacted desires." A moment's reflection grimly clarifies Blake's meaning: to *nurse* an unacted desire is to feed a monster, after already having murdered the cradled infant desire, and the unacted desire, nursed to full size, will be a demon of destruction. The only way out of this cycle of repression and torment is through a perception that transforms time into the eternity of a creative *now,* and that renders space as form until nature itself becomes art. These abstractions are mine, not Blake's, who prefers the more palpable particulars of his Proverbs. "Exuberance is Beauty," and "Where man is not, nature is barren," for exuberance is the stuff of human desire, and the dull round of nature can bear nothing unless man will marry it with the animation of his overflowing energy.

The coda to the Provers of Hell is a brief account of the hardening of poetic myth into priestcraft. The ancient Poets, who were one with the titanic ancient men, animated all sensible objects because they perceived them with "enlarged & numerous senses." The weak in courage, being strong in cunning, chose forms of worship from these poetic tales: "Thus men forgot that All deities reside in the human breast," and thus the contraries of priestly Angels and prophetic Devils sprang into existence.

A Memorable Fancy follows, in which Blake entertains two prophetic predecessors, Isaiah and Ezekiel, at dinner and questions them as to their certainty of being divinely inspired. Isaiah expresses his "firm perswasion" that an honestly indignant human voice is the voice of God, while Ezekiel more directly stresses the necessity for extreme action if the prophet is to raise other men into a perception of the infinite, the human reality that masks as natural appearance.

This prophetic encouragement inspires one of Blake's most passionate perceptions: the natural world is on the point of being purged by fire. The fire here is the fire of intellect and art, which must begin "by an improvement of sensual enjoyment." The active intellect of the artist, raised to its full powers by sexual completion, will consume the whole creation and bring man back to the tree of life, driving away the lesser fire of the guardian cherub's flaming sword. But this sexual completion cannot begin without expunging the pernicious Angelic notion of dualism, and for such work the visionary satirist like Blake is essential. His engraved poems, like the *Marriage,* will be salutary and medicinal corrosives. Even as he creates his plates by melting apparent surfaces away, so the function of his art will be to display the hidden infinite, hid in the phenomenal world. To imitate the artist is to see as he sees:

> If the doors of perception were cleansed every thing would appear
> to man as it is, infinite.
>     For man has closed himself up, till he sees all things thro' narrow
> chinks of his cavern.

This cavern is the skull of fallen man, or in a larger dimension the whole of his fallen body. To see more, we must cleanse the doors of perception we still have, the five senses, but to cleanse them, for Blake, means to begin by raising them to the heights of their sensual power. You do not expand your sense of touch by avoiding sexuality, but only by rising *through* it, and to see more, you must begin by seeing everything you can.

This insistence on the role of increased sensual enjoyment in creation is followed by a sardonic Memorable Fancy confirming that role. Blake is "in a Printing house in Hell," a six-chambered establishment that serves as an allegory of the creative process. In the first chamber is a phallic Dragon-Man "clearing away the rubbish from a cave's mouth," and so cleansing the human sense of touch. Within, other dragons are at work "hollowing the cave," widening the body's potential for imaginative knowledge. Art ensues in this aggressive sexuality, but the next chamber introduces the censorious restrainer, "a Viper folding round the rock & the cave," seeking to confine man within his fallen limits. But a Proverb of Hell comes to our aid: "When thou seest an Eagle, thou seest a portion of Genius; lift up thy head!" So in the next chamber an Eagle combats the Viper by causing "the inside of the cave to be infinite," and the artists who share in a portion of Genius are seen as "numbers of Eagle-like men who built palaces in the immense cliffs." We remember the mighty Devil Blake of an earlier plate, where he hovered on the sides of the rock and wrote sentences in corroding fire. The Eagle-like men prepare us for the fourth chamber of the creative mind, where the archetypes are seen as "Lions of flaming fire, raging around & melting the metals into living fluids." These metals were introduced by the restricting Vipers of reason; now they are melted down into the basic fluids of imaginative life. In the fifth chamber the metals are cast into the expanse of human existence by "Unnam'd forms," who are like the smiths of Yeats's Byzantium. Hell's Printing house ends in a sixth chamber where men take on the forms of books, and the finished creation is at last evident.

These men appear again, in an interlude directly after the Printing house fantasy, as "the Giants who formed this world in its sensual existence, and now seem to live in it in chains." They are our buried energies, our waking appetites, our more than natural resources. Blake now terms them a class of men called the Prolific, and their cunning contrary the class called the Devouring:

> Thus one portion of being is the Prolific, the other the Devouring: To the Devourer it seems as if the producer was in his chains; but it is not so, he only takes portions of existence and fancies that the whole.
>
> But the Prolific would cease to be Prolific unless the Devourer, as a sea, received the excess of his delights.

In this beautiful passage Blake's concept of contraries undergoes a change into a more balanced theory of human existence than was first set forth by "The Voice of the Devil." If ever Blake speaks straight, forgoing all irony, in the *Marriage,* it is here. Reason is still only the outward bound or circumference of Energy, and still fancies that its reductive idea of existence is the whole, rather than a part, of the Human. But the productive Prolific would cease to be itself, would stifle by its own exuberance of invention, if the Devourer ceased to be a primal sea of forms into which the excess of Prolific delights could be received. We are hearing not the Devil's story, and certainly not an Angel's, but the law of human process itself. The Devourer is an outer limit of the Prolific, even as Freud's ego is of his id, but unlike the ego, the Devourer can never manifest itself independently, for Blake will never recognize the validity of a physical world different from the self. Yet the *appearance* of an independent Devourer mocks Blake's Prolific by assuming the shadowy form Blake will later call the Spectre. The process of assumption is remarkably like the constitution of Freud's super-ego, as set forth by Philip Rieff:

> The ego is but an outer portion of the id—crystallizing independently as soon as the infant becomes aware of a physical world different from the self. Then, onto this acceptance of reality lodged in the perceptual system, are superimposed the exhortations of society: first embodied in the figures of the parents and later constituted as a part of the personality, the superego.

As repression is the function of the Devourer, so is it of the Freudian ego. But the Prolific, unlike the id, is not chaotic; it can become chaotic if it lacks all bounds, but this chaos will be an overflux, a superabundance of creativity. By re-stating the contraries as classes of men, Blake has transformed his psychic terms into social ones, and his equivalent of Freud's "civil war" that takes place within the mind now becomes a conflict within culture:

> These two classes of men are always upon earth, & they should be enemies: whoever tries to reconcile them seeks to destroy existence.
> Religion is an endeavour to reconcile the two.

Orthodox religion seeks to transcend the strife of existential contraries by absorbing the Prolific into the Devourer, the energies of men into the organizing categories of the Church. The religious believe that God alone is the Prolific; but Blake is a pragmatic humanist on this issue: "God only Acts and Is, in existing beings or Men." And Blake's Christ, ironically like "Satan or Tempter," is identified in the *Marriage* as another of "the Antediluvians who are our Energies," the Titans repressed by the Sky-gods of reductive reason.

Blake's demonic impiety in making this identification provokes an Angel into commencing the next and longest of the Memorable Fancies, a Swiftian exercise in direct satire. The Angel warns Blake of the dungeon in hell awaiting him. Blake asks to see it:

> So he took me thro' a stable & thro' a church, & down into the church vault, at the end of which was a mill: thro' the mill we went, and came to a cave: down the winding cavern we groped our tedious way, till a void boundless as a nether sky appear'd beneath us, & we held by the roots of trees and hung over this immensity; but I said: "if you please, we will commit ourselves to this void, and see whether providence is here also: if you will not, I will:" but he answer'd: "do not presume, O young man, but as we here remain, behold they lot which will soon appear when the darkness passes away."
> So I remain'd with him, sitting in the twisted root of an oak; he was suspended in a fungus, which hung with the head downward into the deep.

The stable may be either the home of the tamed "horses of instruction" of the Proverb (Foster Damon's suggestion) or simply the stable of Christ's birth, ironically leading into the grander structure of the Church. The vault is emblematic of Christ's burial. In the resurrection of the body Christ passes out of the vault, but the Angel and Blake go to the vault's other end which aptly leads into a mill, mechanical symbol of reductive reason. Once through the mill, and we are in the winding cavern of the fallen mind, in which any groping yields a way that is both downward and tedious, until we hang with Blake and the Angel over the abyss of nature, the unimaginative chaos of reductive intellect. The roots of trees hold us on to the minimal vegetative forms that precariously abide in this mental void. Blake at least has an oak's twisted root for support; his vision paradoxically has a stubborn attachment to natural fact, but the ascetic Angel is properly suspended in a fungus, since those who deny nature for the soul live as parasites *on* the body, not as natural forms within the body. What Blake and the Angel see is the Angelic vision of hell as a torture chamber, complete with a sun giving heat without light, tormenting spiders, and the great Leviathan of Job coming out of the burning East of unrestrained passion, "tinging the black deep with beams of blood, advancing toward us with all the fury of a Spiritual Existence." But the Angel, though a Spiritual Existence himself, climbs back from his fungus into the mill; retreating from this king over all the children of pride into the windings of theology. Left alone, Blake finds that the horrible vision is no more:

> I found myself sitting on a pleasant bank beside a river by moonlight, hearing a harper, who sung to the harp; & his theme was: "The man who never alters his opinion is like standing water, & breeds reptiles of the mind."

The metaphysics of Angels creates Leviathans, but Blake's vision, to which the Angel must now submit, makes monkeys out of theologians:

> "Here," said I, "is your lot, in this space—if space it may be call'd." Soon we saw the stable and the church, & I took him to the altar and open'd the Bible, and lo! it was a deep pit, into which I descended, driving the Angel before me; soon we saw seven houses of brick; one we enter'd; in it were a number of monkeys, baboons, & all of that species, chain'd by the middle, grinning and snatching at one another, but withheld by the shortness of their chains: however, I saw that they sometimes grew numerous, and then the weak were caught by the strong, and with a grinning aspect, first coupled with, & then devour'd, by plucking off first one limb and then another, till the body was left a helpless trunk; this, after grinning & kissing it with seeming fondness, they devour'd too; and here & there I saw one savourily picking the flesh off of his own tail; as the stench terribly annoy'd us both, we went into the mill, and I in my hand brought the skeleton of a body, which in the mill was Aristotle's Analytics.

The "seven houses of brick," as Swinburne surmised, are the seven churches in Asia to whom St. John the Divine addressed his revelation. To reach these temples, Blake takes in his hands Swedenborg's weighty volumes, that Devil and Angel may sink together into the holy void. The gruesome lewdness of Blake's vision of a theological monkey-house has not lost its shock value; it still offends orthodoxy. Swift himself could not have done better here, in the repulsive projection of an incestuous warfare of rival doctrines, ground together in the reductive mill of scholastic priestcraft.

The smack at Swedenborg is sharpened in Blake's next interlude, where we are given an invaluable guide to Blake's notions of cultural precedence:

> Any man of mechanical talents may, from the writings of Paracelsus or Jacob Behmen, produce ten thousand volumes of equal value with Swedenborg's, and from those of Dante or Shakespear an infinite number.
>
> But when he has done this, let him not say that he knows better than his master, for he only holds a candle in sunshine.

This little passage not only dismisses Swedenborg and all systematic reasoners in spiritual matters with him, but quietly implies a truth about Blake that many of his more esoteric scholars might have pondered; Dante and Shakespeare are valued infinitely above the theosophists Paracelsus and Boehme (Behmen), for the great poets are a sunshine in which any mystical writer is only a candle.

The last full section of the *Marriage* is the wisest of its Memorable Fancies, illustrating the Proverb Angels generally will not learn: "Opposition is true Friendship." Blake sees a Devil in a flame of fire rising before an Angel sitting on a cloud. The fire-cloud opposition is premonitory of the symbolic figures into which the Devil and Angel will develop, the fiery Orc of desire and the cloudy Urizen of restraint. Blake's Devil defines the emergent religion of the *Marriage:*

> The worship of God is: Honouring his gifts in other men, each according to his genius, and loving the greatest men best: those who envy or calumniate great men hate God; for there is no other God.

Greatness here means artistic greatness. As God is a Man, for Blake, and finds his being in human acts of creation, so any man who achieves greatness in art is God to the extent of being himself constituted by his own creative acts. The outraged Angel invokes the Ten Commandments and the visibility of God in Jesus Christ, only to hear the Devil proclaim that Jesus was one of the antinomian party:

> I tell you, no virtue can exist without breaking these ten commandments. Jesus was all virtue, and acted from impulse, not from rules.

Blake is resorting again to the rhetoric of shock, as he did at the start of the *Marriage*. As argument, this last Memorable Fancy is weak, but we are not intended to take it as more than a fiery polemic, uttered for its fire and not its light. The Angel at least is drawn to it, embraces the fire, is consumed, and rises again as the archetypal prophet or Devil, Elijah. With an ironic "Note," Blake closes this last section of his gnomic work. The Angel-turned-Devil is the poet's particular friend; together they read the Bible in its infernal or diabolical—that is, in its originally poetic—sense. If the world behaves well, Blake blandly insinuates, they shall have this reading, but in any case they shall receive from Blake "The Bible of Hell," or canon of his engraved poems.

As he works upon writing and engraving the *Marriage*, Blake evidently arrives at the central organizing principle of his life's work. The experiments in pastoral of *Poetical Sketches* and *Songs of Innocence* suggest an emulation of the classical kind of canonical principle, as Blake follows Virgil, Spenser, and Milton in preparing for epic by explorations in man's golden age. But now, in the *Marriage*, Blake declares himself a Biblical poet, in the tradition of the later Milton who repudiated the classical Muses and sought Zion's springs instead. The English Bible, as Blake read it, began with a Creation that was also a Fall, proceeded to the cycle of history, with alternate movements of vision and collapse, and achieved the pastoral art of the Song of Solomon, the tragedy of Job, and the triumphant prophecy of greater poets like Isaiah and Ezekiel. The entrance of this poetry into history in the Gospels was culminated in the Apocalypse, and set a pattern for the Christian poem, a pattern that Milton, in Blake's view, had almost succeeded in emulating.

But the proper poetic use of this pattern, for Blake, depended upon an achieved freedom from the interpretative tradition of priestcraft. The Protestant passion for the Bible as an individual possession, to be read finally by the inner light of each believer's spirit, is Blake's most direct heritage from the radical element in English religious tradition. Blake's Bible of Hell, the sequence of his engraved poems, is the first of the great Romantic displacements of the Biblical revelation into the poetic world of an individual creator, the first of the heterocosms.

Blake chooses not to end the *Marriage* with this promise of his own oncoming world, but with an emblem of the negation of vision. The nightmare of Nebuchadnezzar, fallen from great Babylon down to a dwelling with the beasts of the field, is the nightmare of history unrelieved by the prophet's transforming vision. The *Marriage's* last plate is dominated by a picture of the metamorphized king with the prophecy fulfilled upon him:

The same hour was the thing fulfilled upon Nebuchadnezzar: and he was driven from men, and did eat grass as oxen, and his body was wet with the dew of heaven, till his hairs were grown like eagle's feathers, and his nails like birds' claws.

(Dan. 4:33)

Blake's picture suggests this, and also the great beast of Yeat's *The Second Coming,* with lion body and the head of a man, portending the coming of "mere anarchy" upon the world. Beneath the horror of Nebuchadnezzar, Blake inscribed, as covering Proverb, the dying tyrant Tiriel's gasp of wisdom: "One Law for the Lion & Ox is Oppression." With this outcry against the imposition of any code of uniformity upon contrary individualities, Blake brings *The Marriage of Heaven and Hell* to its proper conclusion. We are left with the memory of the Voice of the Devil, crying aloud in the desert places of a repressive society, and reminding society that it tempts the fate of Nebuchadnezzar, a fall into dazed bestiality, if it will not heed the warnings of vision.

### A Song of Liberty

Engraved in 1792, this vigorous prose poem was associated by Blake with *The Marriage of Heaven and Hell,* to the extent that he sometimes bound it as a coda or pendant to the greater work. In language and conception, *A Song of Liberty* suggests a mature (and politically minded) Rimbaud, exchanging his season in Hell for a summer of unbounded exuberance and imaginative passion. Indeed Blake's *Song* is written in an effective kind of imaginative shorthand, as though the rising enjoyment of poetic fulfillment does not allow time for expansion into even a short romance or prophecy. What Blake gives us is a kind of scenario for an ode of revolutionary triumph. I suspect that *A Song of Liberty* was intended originally as a separate emblem book, in twenty or more plates, and that the twenty numbered sentences of the work were each meant to serve as caption for an individual plate. Certainly each sentence concentrates on a separate image, or an adumbration of an image, until the total image is gathered together in the *Song's* Chorus:

> Let the Priests of the Raven of dawn no longer, in deadly black, with hoarse note curse the sons of joy! Nor his accepted brethren — whom, tyrant, he calls free—lay the bound or build the roof! Nor pale religious letchery call that Virginity that wishes but acts not!
> For everything that lives is Holy!

The Raven of dawn is the sky-god Urizen, associated with the Raven because that is the emblematic bird of Odin, the sky-god of Northern mythology. Urizen's accepted brethren are the vested powers of Europe, who lay the boundary for advancement. Blake would no doubt have disagreed with Bacon's approach to allegory in his *Wisdom of the Ancients* if he had read it, but the fact that Bacon wrote such a book at all makes it difficult to dismiss him as a mere Philistine whose "first principle is Unbelief." Locke's virile contempt of slavery, his defense of toleration, and even the primacy he gives to sense experience in his theory of knowledge are all Blakean qualities. Newton's work in science certainly did not make him a "Deist"; he had an interest in apocalyptic thought which deserved something better, from Blake's point of view, than the ridicule which Blake seems to give it. Not one of these thinkers are as opposed to Blake's mode of thought as, for instance, Hobbes, whom he never mentions, where there are barriers against Blake's apocalyptic humanism far more rigid than anything his three favorite antagonists erect.

Now whether Blake had read Hobbes or not, he is by no means unaware of the force of this objection. But we have already seen how important to Blake is the Baconian principle that truth comes more readily from error than from confusion. What Blake most fears and hates is more easily defended by hypocrisy or self-deception than by frankness. "Truth," he says, "can never be told so as to be understood, and not be believ'd." The inference is that falsehood can never be told so as to be understood, and not be recognized as false. The very honesty of Hobbes lets the tyrant's cat, or rather Leviathan, out of the bag. It is the reasonable and persuasive Locke who is likely to attract a well-meaning audience, and it is far more important to attack him than Hobbes, who could be plausibly denounced by even a stupid or malicious person. Similarly, though predestination was a doctrine Blake loathed, he does not attack it in Augustine or Calvin; he attacks a tendency to it in his master Swedenborg. Again, the Deist belief that an idea of God is innate in man is in a sense closer to Blake than it is to Locke, who denies it, and certainly closer than atheism is. But Blake saw in Deism, not atheism, the really pernicious foe of Christianity.

This idea that truth in a false context is worse than outspoken falsehood leads in Blake's thought to a distinction between a "contrary" and a "negation." In society the contraries are the "Devils" and the "Angels" already mentioned. Blake and Locke are contraries: both feel that imagination, liberty and life are in their systems, and they must clash or we shall never know who is right. Hobbes is a negation: he cares too little for imagination or liberty to clash with any defender of it. In *Milton* Blake calls the negations "the Elect from before the foundation of the world," an ironic reference to the theory of predestination. They are the Pharisees who turn all religion, Jewish, Christian or Deist, into a routine of ritual and morality. They are the righteous whom Jesus did *not* call to repentance, and of whom he says with grim ambiguous irony: "They have their reward." The contraries Blake calls the "Reprobate" and the "Redeemed": they correspond to Rintrah and Palamabron. The former are the persecuted and

man's liberty and build the roof of the orthodox heaven above man's head. The whiteness of religious chastity is the paleness of sexual repression, murderously nursing unacted desires. But all true desire is sacred, for everything that *lives* is holy. A *Song of Liberty* reaches this conclusion by a rhapsodic mythic narrative that outlines the main characters and events of more finished prophetic poems by Blake. In attaching it to *The Marriage of Heaven and Hell,* Blake provides us with an introduction to poems like *Visions of the Daughters of Albion, America, Europe,* and *The Book of Urizen.*

A *Song of Liberty* begins with the groaning in childbirth of an Eternal Female, later to be named Enitharmon, the Queen of Heaven. She is giving birth to a "new born fire," Orc, a muttering shiver among the tyrannies of Europe, for the temporal manifestation of this fire is the French Revolution. But the "new born terror" is not powerful enough to overcome Urizen, "the starry king":

8. On those infinite mountains of light, now barr'd out by the Atlantic sea, the new-born fire stood before the starry king!

Blake is introducing his version of the myth of lost Atlantis, later to be developed in *America.* The confrontation between Orc and Urizen takes place in the unfallen world, from which we are separated by the Atlantic, chaotic sea and sinister emblem of our minimal notions of space and time. Orc seems to lose the battle, and like Lucifer is hurled down flaming into the abyss. But the falling fire makes an ironic appearance on earth as the Revolution, the active springing from energy that seems diabolical to orthodox society.

Urizen and his host fall also, so that Blake's version of Milton's Fall of the Angels brings down both Jehovah-Urizen and Lucifer-Orc. With fine irony, Blake parallels Urizen's gathering together of his forces with Satan's rallying of his host in *Paradise Lost.* In a more daring analogue, worthy of the Bible of Hell, the figure of Moses is invoked as the next stage in Urizen's career:

18. With thunder and fire, leading his starry hosts thro' the waste wilderness, he promulgates his ten commands, glancing his beamy eyelids over the deep in dark dismay,
19. Where the son of fire in his eastern cloud, while the morning plumes her golden breast,
20. Spurning the clouds written with curses, stamps the stony law to dust, loosing the eternal horses from the dens of night, crying: EMPIRE IS NO MORE! AND NOW THE LION & WOLF SHALL CEASE.

The Ten Commandments are set here in the most negative of contexts, and their close association with Empire marks the passage as one of the most antinomian in Blake. Yet even at his most turbulent and rebellious, Blake does not altogether forget the necessity of contraries. The dens of night, from which Orc looses the horses, releasing them from Instruction to Wrath, are referred to earlier in *A Song of Liberty* as "Urthona's dens," where Urizen and his starry host lie all night beneath the ruins. Urthona is the unfallen or eternal name of the being who will evolve into the hero of Blake's myth, Los, the imaginative shaper who must be the agent of a human apocalypse. To be in Urthona's dens is to have fallen into the lowest regions of creativity, and yet to be still within a possibility of further creation. *A Song of Liberty* therefore does not simply describe a conflict between tyrannizing restraint and revolutionary desire, with all our sympathies given to desire, but hints at the conflict as being a clash of creative forces, blindly striving against a background that Blake has yet to clarify.

# The Thief of Fire

*Northrop Frye*

Once we begin to look at Blake's engraved works as a canon, we certain structural principles within it. *The Marriage of Heaven and H* of which is fundamentally that of a prose satire, rises out of the r "minor prophecies" in a class by itself. But there are three poems wl dently intended to form a single group: *America, Europe* and *The* the last of these being divided into two parts called respectively " "Asia." *America* is clearly a revolutionary poem; so is "Asia," and s poem on the French Revolution, which was never engraved. These and *The Marriage of Heaven and Hell* revolve around the character v calls Orc, and are concerned, like a good deal of Milton's prose, wi connection of three themes: the theme of satire, or the prophet's c of society; the theme of achieving liberty through revolutionary act theme of apocalypse. We begin with the theme of satire.

It has doubtless occurred to the reader already that Bacon, Newtc do not look very convincing in the role of three-headed hellish Cer Blake assigns them. It is not so much that Blake is unfair to them a thinker should be judged by the quality of his influence as well as views. That is, it is an error of fact to call Locke a Deist, but it is of interpretation to see many affinities between Deism and Locke knowledge. But Blake's unfairness is more extreme than that. Afte had a profound respect for the imaginative communication of truth and parable, and if it does not bulk large in *The Advancement of Lea* only because he considered that poetry was doing fairly well an

From *Fearful Symmetry: A Study of William Blake.* © 1947 by Princeton Univer outcast prophets; the latter are the timid well-meaning orthodox whose good qualities emerge only after the prophets have hammered their timidity to pieces. The clash of contraries is thus an essential part of the "redemption" of mankind. In *The Marriage of Heaven and Hell* a "Devil" makes a violent attack on an "Angel," who becomes converted. "This Angel," says Blake, "who is now become a Devil, is my particular friend." Similarly, in the final consummation of the world portrayed in *Jerusalem*, we see "the innumerable Chariots of the Almighty"—

"And Bacon & Newton & Locke, & Milton & Shakspear & Chaucer"

taking equal place in the vision.

The same distinction between a contrary and a negation occurs in Blake's theory of ideas. All real things have qualities in them, and qualities always have opposites. This is particularly true of moral qualities, as every virtue has its corresponding vice. All "good" men by any standards may be "bad" by other standards, just as an egg that is bad to eat may be good to throw at someone. But the believer in the cloven fiction prefers to identify a real thing with one of its qualities, because things become easier to generalize about when classified into qualities. Now as things are good or bad according to circumstances, the cloven fiction leads to the absolutizing of circumstances. The deader a thing is, the more obedient it is to circumstances, and the more alive it is the less predictable it becomes. Hence the believer in the cloven fiction finds it much easier to understand the behavior of dead things, the objects of exact science under the law of "mathematic form." And in studying human activity he again finds it easiest to understand when it is most automatic. So insensibly he tends to call "the passive that obeys Reason" good, and "the active springing from Energy" bad. The result is that illegitimate pun on the word "law" which associates a description of a predictable process in nature with the definition of an ideal standard of human conduct:

And this is the manner of the Sons of Albion in their strength:
They take the Two Contraries which are call'd Qualities, with
    which
Every Substance is clothed: they name them Good & Evil
From them they make an Abstract, which is a Negation
Not only of the Substance from which it is derived,
A murderer of its own Body, but also a murderer
Of every Divine Member: it is the Reasoning Power,
An Abstract objecting power that Negatives every thing.

In society, the contraries and negation are the reprobate visionary, the elected tyrant and the victim whom the visionary has to redeem. This means that the victim, not the tyrant, is the prophet's contrary, and the object of his attack.

The source of all tyranny is the mental passivity induced by abstract reasoning in the victim's mind, and until that is got rid of all rulers will be compelled to be tyrants. "The tygers of wrath are wiser than the horses of instruction": the glittering intensity of prophetic vision sees its real prey in the stupid, blinkered vision that distorts forms into frightening monsters.

We may push this opposition of visionary and reasoner a little further. Blake assigns to Aristotle the dictum that "Characters are either Good or Bad," and comments, "A Horse is not more a Lion for being a Bad Horse: that is its Character: its Goodness or Badness is another consideration." To the artist a horse's character is its form: he may make a perfectly good use of what would in other respects be a bad horse, as Cervantes did of Rozinante, and he has no further interest in its goodness or badness. The moralist or reasoner, on the other hand (the two words are synonyms in Blake: we shall see why presently), will select certain forms of behavior and reject others: denounce this and commend that. He will not understand what "use" an artist can make of anything except in relation to choosing what he calls "good" and avoiding what he calls "bad"; and if he had his own way with the arts, he would censor and expurgate along these lines. It is necessary then for art to have some line of defense against theoretical invasions. Such a line of defense would naturally be a satire directed against the pretenses of the reasoning moralist.

Hence there is frequently an antiphilosophical bias in satire, and the literary precedents for Blake's attack on Bacon, Newton and Locke in English literature are the attacks of Samuel Butler and Swift on Cartesian logic and Royal Society virtuosi. We could see this more clearly if Blake had selected, say, Descartes for his target instead of the three Englishmen. Of course Butler and Swift are equally merciless on an occult tradition for which Blake had more sympathy, but still *The Marriage of Heaven and Hell* (which incidentally gives quite a rough ride to Swedenborg) is closer to them than to the occultists. For the hostility to science and philosophy displayed in the Laputa section of *Gulliver's Travels* and *The Elephant in the Moon* is neither irresponsible nor incidental: it springs from the artist's insistence that the totality of experience is far greater than all attempts to summarize it in formulas. The scientists in *The Elephant in the Moon* who deliberately rule out inconvenient evidence are not simply dishonest men: there would be little point in the satire if they were. They symbolize the scientific preoccupation with the small part of life capable of logical and experimental treatment. Such preoccupation, according to Blake, is oversimplified and in the long run inhuman, and he charges the "reasoner" with a self-absorbed introspection only one remove from schizophrenia. He is anticipated in Swift's portrayal of the scientific dignitaries of Laputa who need flappers to recall them to the world. . . .

The central idea of *The Marriage of Heaven and Hell*, to put it crudely, is that the unrest which has produced the French and American revolutions indicates that the end of the world might come at any time. The end of the world, the apocalypse, is the objective counterpart of the resurrection of man, his return to the titanic bodily form he originally possessed. When we say that man has fallen, we mean that his soul has collapsed into the form of the body in which he now exists. Hence, while no one could be less of an ascetic than Blake, the premise from which the ascetic starts is also his. The body is "vile": it is the body of a peeled ape, a witch's cauldron of tangled tissues and sodden excrement cooking in blood. This is as true of the nightingale as it is of the vulture, and as true of the tender virgin as it is of the gorilla. The physical nausea so painfully developed in Swift is an example of a soul's disgusted reaction to its degraded state. But where the ascetics go wrong is in forgetting that all mental activity is also a bodily struggle, because based on sense experience. The prophecies resound with bitter complaints of the inadequacy of the body, of the impotence of the eye to see and of the nose to smell, but the moral in Blake is that the body is weak enough already without trying to split it in two. Now we cannot by taking thought add a cubit to our statures; it is a change of worlds that is necessary, the lifting of the whole body to a fully imaginative plane by getting rid of the natural man.

The transformation of the body into a spiritual substance is the Christian doctrine of bodily ressurection. Job puts this doctrine in the form of its essential paradox: "And though after my skin worms destroy this body, yet in my flesh shall I see God." There is no soul imprisoned within the body evaporating at death, but a living man armed with all the powers of his present body, infinitely expanded. The relation of soul to body is that of an oak to an acorn, not of a genie to a bottle. And there are no natural laws which the risen body must obey and no compulsory categories by which it must perceive. It is impossible to picture this except in terms of what we now see, and providing angels with wings is about as far as we can get. As Blake says, "From a perception of only 3 senses or 3 elements none could deduce fourth or fifth"; and we have no idea how many imaginative powers we do not possess. But Jesus, says Paul:

> shall change our vile body, that it may be fashioned like unto his
> glorious body, according to the working whereby he is able even
> to subdue all things unto himself.

*Esse est percipi,* and because we perceive on the level of this body we see an independent nature in a looming and sinister perspective. We are still living in an age of giant stars just as the ants are still living in an age of giant ferns; the natural man is a mole, and all our mountains are his molehills. In the resurrection of the body the physical universe would take the form in which it would be perceived by the risen body, and the risen body would perceive it in the form of Paradise.

The complete conquest of nature implied by the words "resurrection" and "apocalypse" is a mystery bound up with the end of time, but not with death. When the Selfhood is asked what it wants to do, it can only answer, with the Sibyl in Petronius, that it wants to die, and it thinks of death as a resolution. To the imagination physical death isolates the part that lives in the spiritual world; but as that world is the real here and the real now, we do not have to wait to die to live in it. "Whenever any Individual Rejects Error & Embraces Truth, a Last Judgment passes upon that Individual." Similarly, the apocalypse could occur at any time in history if men wanted it badly enough to stop playing their silly game of hide-and-seek with nature. Visionaries, artists, prophets and martyrs all live as though an apocalypse were around the corner, and without this sense of a potentially imminent crisis imagination loses most of its driving power. The expectation of a Last Judgment in the New Testament does not mean that the Christians of that time were victims of a mass delusion, or that they were hypnotizing themselves in order to nerve themselves for martyrdom, but that they saw the physical universe as precariously balanced on the mental cowardice of man. And when Blake and Milton elaborate theories of history suggesting that time is reaching its final crisis during their own lives, they are only doing what Jesus did before them.

The resurrection of the body means the resurrection of all the body, and as the physical body has a sexual origin, the sexual life, Blake says, becomes a human one, which means that sex is transformed, not eliminated. In eternity, Blake remarks dryly:

> Embraces are Cominglings from the Head even to the Feet,
> And not a pompous High Priest entering by a Secret Place.

That is why in the Bible the apocalypse is often referred to as a wedding, a union in love in which the relation of man to nature becomes the relation of the lover to the beloved, the Bridegroom to the Bride. And as the Bride in Blake is Jerusalem, a city in Eden and a "married land" in Beulah, it is in Beulah that the sexual aspect of life becomes fulfilled. But Beulah is the state of existence directly above our own, hence the apocalypse will begin by "an improvement of sensual enjoyment"—Blake uses the adjective deliberately.

And as the risen body perceives the new world the old one perishes in flames. Why flames? Because fire is the greatest possible combination in this world of heat and light, and the risen body lives in the greatest possible combination of the spiritual forms of heat and light: energy or desire, and reason or vision. Fire destroys the solid form of nature, and those who have believed nature to be solid will find themselves in a lake of fire at the *Dies Irae*. But the imagination cannot be consumed by fire, for it is fire; the burning bush of God which never exhausts its material. It is this fire that "delights in its form."

The word "consummation," often applied to the apocalypse, refers both to the burning world and the sacred marriage. Paradise itself is a place of flaming fire, the fires being the "lustful" passions which there are fully gratified. They are also "thought-creating fires" because gratified desire produces reason. Eden is a fiery city, as is indicated in Ezekiel's speech to the Covering Cherub: "Thou hast been in Eden the garden of God . . . thou hast walked up and down in the midst of the stones of fire." Similarly the three whom Nebuchadnezzar put into a fiery furnace were seen to be walking unhurt in the fire with the Son of God.

Since the Fall, there has been a flaming sword over Paradise, and fire is now something to be approached with more circumspection. Orthodox theology tells us that in the eternal world the fires of hell have heat without light, and that heaven is a blaze of golden light, the question of heat being slurred over. Remembering that passion and desire are spiritual heat, such doctrines tell us symbolically that desires are hellish and that we shall be tortured forever for having them, whereas those who have emasculated their passions will be admitted to a heaven in which the kind of divine love they enjoy, while its exact nature is unknown, is certain to be something very, very pure. Like forest animals, the orthodox have a fascinated horror of fire and its torments, and when we come down to the skeptical obscurantism of the "new philosophy," "the element of fire is quite put out." What is coming is the union of heat and light, a marriage of heaven and hell. By "hell" Blake means an upsurge of desire and passion within the rising body so great that it will destroy the present starry heaven, and he calls it "hell" because that is what the orthodox call it. Here Blake's meaning has been misunderstood, and deserves more explanation.

Everything that furthers and increases the creative life is really good. The growth of creative energy is the tree of life which enables men to attain an eternal existence. Whatever is pleasing to society, whatever is cautious, prudent and undistinguished, or else vicious and cruel if society happens to be feeling that way, is morally good. The growth of morality is the tree of the knowledge of good and evil which leads to death. The former is the gospel; the latter the "law" under which all non-Christians, and most of the nominal Christians, live. Michael explains to Adam in *Paradise Lost* that it is the business of the law to discover sin rather than remove it. Moral good and moral evil do not represent any genuine opposition. The one wages wars and executes criminals; the other murders. The one exploits labor; the other robs. The one establishes marriage on the destruction of virginity; the other rapes. But they have a common enemy, the power of genius and prophecy. In terms of moral good it is not the murderer or the robber but the prophet who is really evil. Barabbas may be safely released, for it is impossible that his robberies can destroy the social structure of Pilate and Caiaphas; but there is deadly danger in Jesus and John the Baptist, who must be got rid of at all costs.

That is why no one can be saved by moral virtue. But it does not follow that Barabbas is in a higher imaginative state than Caiaphas. This takes us back by another road to our distinction of contrary and negation. The criminal is not the contrary but the negation of the morally good man; he breaks the law, but he has no gospel. And though the prophet is regarded by society as a devil or messenger from hell, he never practises the vice of "hindering another." There is much that is really good in moral good: the prophet is concerned only to disentangle it from the easy virtue of moral cowardice.

*The Marriage of Heaven and Hell,* therefore, has nothing to do with the simple inversion of moral good and evil which is known as sadism, and which forms an important aspect of Romantic culture. This is a traditional error in the interpretation of Blake, and one which ignores the fact that Blake attaches two meanings to the word "hell," one real and the other ironic. There is a real hell in the human mind, and it achieves the physical form of dungeons, whips, racks and all the miserable panoply of fear. Such a hell consolidates a moral virtue founded on terror with a moral evil founded on cruelty, and it exists because it is believed to be a part of "necessity." The more degenerate the society, the more obvious this alliance of moral good and evil against the power of genius becomes. Those who know better can see that, as evil is a negation, this hell would be, in the spiritual world, nothingness, a monstrous multiple of zero. No one could go on living in it after the Last Judgment, because no one can exist in a state of nonexistence, the post-apocalyptic hell of unending torment being, like the fallen sun, "a phantasy of evil Man." Whatever foreshadows the Last Judgment thus foreshadows the annihilation of hell, and of the believers in it who are negations, "the Elect from before the foundation of the world," and can have no existence after those foundations have disappeared. Hence for these "Elect" anything which makes persecution and oppression seem less "necessary," that is, any blow struck for human freedom, is their hell, and the announcement of a new hope, a new courage, a new faith and a new vision is, to them, "the voice of the devil." The darkness does not comprehend the light; evil spirits fade on the crowing of the cock, and from their point of view it is the cock that is the evil spirit, the herald of the light which afflicts them with the "frantic pain" of the spirit in the "Mad Song."

We have more definite evidence for the same point in *The Ghost of Abel,* which is addressed to Byron and is apparently conceived as an answer to that poet's *Cain.* Cain is provided by Byron with a great deal of imaginative vision.

man's liberty and build the roof of the orthodox heaven above man's head. The whiteness of religious chastity is the paleness of sexual repression, murderously nursing unacted desires. But all true desire is sacred, for everything that *lives* is holy. *A Song of Liberty* reaches this conclusion by a rhapsodic mythic narrative that outlines the main characters and events of more finished prophetic poems by Blake. In attaching it to *The Marriage of Heaven and Hell,* Blake provides us with an introduction to poems like *Visions of the Daughters of Albion, America, Europe,* and *The Book of Urizen.*

*A Song of Liberty* begins with the groaning in childbirth of an Eternal Female, later to be named Enitharmon, the Queen of Heaven. She is giving birth to a "new born fire," Orc, a muttering shiver among the tyrannies of Europe, for the temporal manifestation of this fire is the French Revolution. But the "new born terror" is not powerful enough to overcome Urizen, "the starry king":

> 8. On those infinite mountains of light, now barr'd out by the Atlantic
> sea, the new-born fire stood before the starry king!

Blake is introducing his version of the myth of lost Atlantis, later to be developed in *America.* The confrontation between Orc and Urizen takes place in the unfallen world, from which we are separated by the Atlantic, chaotic sea and sinister emblem of our minimal notions of space and time. Orc seems to lose the battle, and like Lucifer is hurled down flaming into the abyss. But the falling fire makes an ironic appearance on earth as the Revolution, the active springing from energy that seems diabolical to orthodox society.

Urizen and his host fall also, so that Blake's version of Milton's Fall of the Angels brings down both Jehovah-Urizen and Lucifer-Orc. With fine irony, Blake parallels Urizen's gathering together of his forces with Satan's rallying of his host in *Paradise Lost.* In a more daring analogue, worthy of the Bible of Hell, the figure of Moses is invoked as the next stage in Urizen's career:

> 18. With thunder and fire, leading his starry hosts thro' the waste
> wilderness, he promulgates his ten commands, glancing his beamy
> eyelids over the deep in dark dismay,
> 19. Where the son of fire in his eastern cloud, while the morning
> plumes her golden breast,
> 20. Spurning the clouds written with curses, stamps the stony law
> to dust, loosing the eternal horses from the dens of night, crying:
> EMPIRE IS NO MORE! AND NOW THE LION & WOLF SHALL CEASE.

The Ten Commandments are set here in the most negative of contexts, and their close association with Empire marks the passage as one of the most antinomian in Blake. Yet even at his most turbulent and rebellious, Blake does not altogether forget the necessity of contraries. The dens of night, from which Orc looses the horses, releasing them from Instruction to Wrath, are referred to earlier in *A Song of Liberty* as "Urthona's dens," where Urizen and his starry host lie all night beneath the ruins. Urthona is the unfallen or eternal name of the being who will evolve into the hero of Blake's myth, Los, the imaginative shaper who must be the agent of a human apocalypse. To be in Urthona's dens is to have fallen into the lowest regions of creativity, and yet to be still within a possibility of further creation. *A Song of Liberty* therefore does not simply describe a conflict between tyrannizing restraint and revolutionary desire, with all our sympathies given to desire, but hints at the conflict as being a clash of creative forces, blindly striving against a background that Blake has yet to clarify.

# The Thief of Fire

*Northrop Frye*

Once we begin to look at Blake's engraved works as a canon, we can discern certain structural principles within it. *The Marriage of Heaven and Hell,* the form of which is fundamentally that of a prose satire, rises out of the midst of the "minor prophecies" in a class by itself. But there are three poems which are evidently intended to form a single group: *America, Europe* and *The Song of Los,* the last of these being divided into two parts called respectively "Africa" and "Asia." *America* is clearly a revolutionary poem; so is "Asia," and so is another poem on the French Revolution, which was never engraved. These four poems and *The Marriage of Heaven and Hell* revolve around the character whom Blake calls Orc, and are concerned, like a good deal of Milton's prose, with the interconnection of three themes: the theme of satire, or the prophet's denunciation of society; the theme of achieving liberty through revolutionary action; and the theme of apocalypse. We begin with the theme of satire.

It has doubtless occurred to the reader already that Bacon, Newton and Locke do not look very convincing in the role of three-headed hellish Cerberus which Blake assigns them. It is not so much that Blake is unfair to them personally: a thinker should be judged by the quality of his influence as well as by his own views. That is, it is an error of fact to call Locke a Deist, but it is not an error of interpretation to see many affinities between Deism and Locke's theory of knowledge. But Blake's unfairness is more extreme than that. After all, Bacon had a profound respect for the imaginative communication of truth in allegory and parable, and if it does not bulk large in *The Advancement of Learning,* it was only because he considered that poetry was doing fairly well and needed no

---

From *Fearful Symmetry: A Study of William Blake.* © 1947 by Princeton University Press.

advancement. Blake would no doubt have disagreed with Bacon's approach to allegory in his *Wisdom of the Ancients* if he had read it, but the fact that Bacon wrote such a book at all makes it difficult to dismiss him as a mere Philistine whose "first principle is Unbelief." Locke's virile contempt of slavery, his defense of toleration, and even the primacy he gives to sense experience in his theory of knowledge are all Blakean qualities. Newton's work in science certainly did not make him a "Deist"; he had an interest in apocalyptic thought which deserved something better, from Blake's point of view, than the ridicule which Blake seems to give it. Not one of these thinkers are as opposed to Blake's mode of thought as, for instance, Hobbes, whom he never mentions, where there are barriers against Blake's apocalyptic humanism far more rigid than anything his three favorite antagonists erect.

Now whether Blake had read Hobbes or not, he is by no means unaware of the force of this objection. But we have already seen how important to Blake is the Baconian principle that truth comes more readily from error than from confusion. What Blake most fears and hates is more easily defended by hypocrisy or self-deception than by frankness. "Truth," he says, "can never be told so as to be understood, and not be believ'd." The inference is that falsehood can never be told so as to be understood, and not be recognized as false. The very honesty of Hobbes lets the tyrant's cat, or rather Leviathan, out of the bag. It is the reasonable and persuasive Locke who is likely to attract a well-meaning audience, and it is far more important to attack him than Hobbes, who could be plausibly denounced by even a stupid or malicious person. Similarly, though predestination was a doctrine Blake loathed, he does not attack it in Augustine or Calvin; he attacks a tendency to it in his master Swedenborg. Again, the Deist belief that an idea of God is innate in man is in a sense closer to Blake than it is to Locke, who denies it, and certainly closer than atheism is. But Blake saw in Deism, not atheism, the really pernicious foe of Christianity.

This idea that truth in a false context is worse than outspoken falsehood leads in Blake's thought to a distinction between a "contrary" and a "negation." In society the contraries are the "Devils" and the "Angels" already mentioned. Blake and Locke are contraries: both feel that imagination, liberty and life are in their systems, and they must clash or we shall never know who is right. Hobbes is a negation: he cares too little for imagination or liberty to clash with any defender of it. In *Milton* Blake calls the negations "the Elect from before the foundation of the world," an ironic reference to the theory of predestination. They are the Pharisees who turn all religion, Jewish, Christian or Deist, into a routine of ritual and morality. They are the righteous whom Jesus did *not* call to repentance, and of whom he says with grim ambiguous irony: "They have their reward." The contraries Blake calls the "Reprobate" and the "Redeemed": they correspond to Rintrah and Palamabron. The former are the persecuted and outcast prophets; the latter are the timid well-meaning orthodox whose good qualities emerge only after the prophets have hammered their timidity to pieces. The clash of contraries is thus an essential part of the "redemption" of mankind. In *The Marriage of Heaven and Hell* a "Devil" makes a violent attack on an "Angel," who becomes converted. "This Angel," says Blake, "who is now become a Devil, is my particular friend." Similarly, in the final consummation of the world portrayed in *Jerusalem*, we see "the innumerable Chariots of the Almighty"—

"And Bacon & Newton & Locke, & Milton & Shakspear & Chaucer"

taking equal place in the vision.

The same distinction between a contrary and a negation occurs in Blake's theory of ideas. All real things have qualities in them, and qualities always have opposites. This is particularly true of moral qualities, as every virtue has its corresponding vice. All "good" men by any standards may be "bad" by other standards, just as an egg that is bad to eat may be good to throw at someone. But the believer in the cloven fiction prefers to identify a real thing with one of its qualities, because things become easier to generalize about when classified into qualities. Now as things are good or bad according to circumstances, the cloven fiction leads to the absolutizing of circumstances. The deader a thing is, the more obedient it is to circumstances, and the more alive it is the less predictable it becomes. Hence the believer in the cloven fiction finds it much easier to understand the behavior of dead things, the objects of exact science under the law of "mathematic form." And in studying human activity he again finds it easiest to understand when it is most automatic. So insensibly he tends to call "the passive that obeys Reason" good, and "the active springing from Energy" bad. The result is that illegitimate pun on the word "law" which associates a description of a predictable process in nature with the definition of an ideal standard of human conduct:

> And this is the manner of the Sons of Albion in their strength:
> They take the Two Contraries which are call'd Qualities, with
>     which
> Every Substance is clothed: they name them Good & Evil
> From them they make an Abstract, which is a Negation
> Not only of the Substance from which it is derived,
> A murderer of its own Body, but also a murderer
> Of every Divine Member: it is the Reasoning Power,
> An Abstract objecting power that Negatives every thing.

In society, the contraries and negation are the reprobate visionary, the elected tyrant and the victim whom the visionary has to redeem. This means that the victim, not the tyrant, is the prophet's contrary, and the object of his attack.

The source of all tyranny is the mental passivity induced by abstract reasoning in the victim's mind, and until that is got rid of all rulers will be compelled to be tyrants. "The tygers of wrath are wiser than the horses of instruction": the glittering intensity of prophetic vision sees its real prey in the stupid, blinkered vision that distorts forms into frightening monsters.

We may push this opposition of visionary and reasoner a little further. Blake assigns to Aristotle the dictum that "Characters are either Good or Bad," and comments, "A Horse is not more a Lion for being a Bad Horse: that is its Character: its Goodness or Badness is another consideration." To the artist a horse's character is its form: he may make a perfectly good use of what would in other respects be a bad horse, as Cervantes did of Rozinante, and he has no further interest in its goodness or badness. The moralist or reasoner, on the other hand (the two words are synonyms in Blake: we shall see why presently), will select certain forms of behavior and reject others: denounce this and commend that. He will not understand what "use" an artist can make of anything except in relation to choosing what he calls "good" and avoiding what he calls "bad"; and if he had his own way with the arts, he would censor and expurgate along these lines. It is necessary then for art to have some line of defense against theoretical invasions. Such a line of defense would naturally be a satire directed against the pretenses of the reasoning moralist.

Hence there is frequently an antiphilosophical bias in satire, and the literary precedents for Blake's attack on Bacon, Newton and Locke in English literature are the attacks of Samuel Butler and Swift on Cartesian logic and Royal Society virtuosi. We could see this more clearly if Blake had selected, say, Descartes for his target instead of the three Englishmen. Of course Butler and Swift are equally merciless on an occult tradition for which Blake had more sympathy, but still *The Marriage of Heaven and Hell* (which incidentally gives quite a rough ride to Swedenborg) is closer to them than to the occultists. For the hostility to science and philosophy displayed in the Laputa section of *Gulliver's Travels* and *The Elephant in the Moon* is neither irresponsible nor incidental: it springs from the artist's insistence that the totality of experience is far greater than all attempts to summarize it in formulas. The scientists in *The Elephant in the Moon* who deliberately rule out inconvenient evidence are not simply dishonest men: there would be little point in the satire if they were. They symbolize the scientific preoccupation with the small part of life capable of logical and experimental treatment. Such preoccupation, according to Blake, is oversimplified and in the long run inhuman, and he charges the "reasoner" with a self-absorbed introspection only one remove from schizophrenia. He is anticipated in Swift's portrayal of the scientific dignitaries of Laputa who need flappers to recall them to the world. . . .

The central idea of *The Marriage of Heaven and Hell,* to put it crudely, is that the unrest which has produced the French and American revolutions indicates that the end of the world might come at any time. The end of the world, the apocalypse, is the objective counterpart of the resurrection of man, his return to the titanic bodily form he originally possessed. When we say that man has fallen, we mean that his soul has collapsed into the form of the body in which he now exists. Hence, while no one could be less of an ascetic than Blake, the premise from which the ascetic starts is also his. The body is "vile": it is the body of a peeled ape, a witch's cauldron of tangled tissues and sodden excrement cooking in blood. This is as true of the nightingale as it is of the vulture, and as true of the tender virgin as it is of the gorilla. The physical nausea so painfully developed in Swift is an example of a soul's disgusted reaction to its degraded state. But where the ascetics go wrong is in forgetting that all mental activity is also a bodily struggle, because based on sense experience. The prophecies resound with bitter complaints of the inadequacy of the body, of the impotence of the eye to see and of the nose to smell, but the moral in Blake is that the body is weak enough already without trying to split it in two. Now we cannot by taking thought add a cubit to our statures; it is a change of worlds that is necessary, the lifting of the whole body to a fully imaginative plane by getting rid of the natural man.

The transformation of the body into a spiritual substance is the Christian doctrine of bodily ressurection. Job puts this doctrine in the form of its essential paradox: "And though after my skin worms destroy this body, yet in my flesh shall I see God." There is no soul imprisoned within the body evaporating at death, but a living man armed with all the powers of his present body, infinitely expanded. The relation of soul to body is that of an oak to an acorn, not of a genie to a bottle. And there are no natural laws which the risen body must obey and no compulsory categories by which it must perceive. It is impossible to picture this except in terms of what we now see, and providing angels with wings is about as far as we can get. As Blake says, "From a perception of only 3 senses or 3 elements none could deduce fourth or fifth"; and we have no idea how many imaginative powers we do not possess. But Jesus, says Paul:

> shall change our vile body, that it may be fashioned like unto his
> glorious body, according to the working whereby he is able even
> to subdue all things unto himself.

*Esse est percipi,* and because we perceive on the level of this body we see an independent nature in a looming and sinister perspective. We are still living in an age of giant stars just as the ants are still living in an age of giant ferns; the natural man is a mole, and all our mountains are his molehills. In the resurrection of the body the physical universe would take the form in which it would be perceived by the risen body, and the risen body would perceive it in the form of Paradise.

The complete conquest of nature implied by the words "resurrection" and "apocalypse" is a mystery bound up with the end of time, but not with death. When the Selfhood is asked what it wants to do, it can only answer, with the Sibyl in Petronius, that it wants to die, and it thinks of death as a resolution. To the imagination physical death isolates the part that lives in the spiritual world; but as that world is the real here and the real now, we do not have to wait to die to live in it. "Whenever any Individual Rejects Error & Embraces Truth, a Last Judgment passes upon that Individual." Similarly, the apocalypse could occur at any time in history if men wanted it badly enough to stop playing their silly game of hide-and-seek with nature. Visionaries, artists, prophets and martyrs all live as though an apocalypse were around the corner, and without this sense of a potentially imminent crisis imagination loses most of its driving power. The expectation of a Last Judgment in the New Testament does not mean that the Christians of that time were victims of a mass delusion, or that they were hypnotizing themselves in order to nerve themselves for martyrdom, but that they saw the physical universe as precariously balanced on the mental cowardice of man. And when Blake and Milton elaborate theories of history suggesting that time is reaching its final crisis during their own lives, they are only doing what Jesus did before them.

The resurrection of the body means the resurrection of all the body, and as the physical body has a sexual origin, the sexual life, Blake says, becomes a human one, which means that sex is transformed, not eliminated. In eternity, Blake remarks dryly:

> Embraces are Cominglings from the Head even to the Feet,
> And not a pompous High Priest entering by a Secret Place.

That is why in the Bible the apocalypse is often referred to as a wedding, a union in love in which the relation of man to nature becomes the relation of the lover to the beloved, the Bridegroom to the Bride. And as the Bride in Blake is Jerusalem, a city in Eden and a "married land" in Beulah, it is in Beulah that the sexual aspect of life becomes fulfilled. But Beulah is the state of existence directly above our own, hence the apocalypse will begin by "an improvement of sensual enjoyment"—Blake uses the adjective deliberately.

And as the risen body perceives the new world the old one perishes in flames. Why flames? Because fire is the greatest possible combination in this world of heat and light, and the risen body lives in the greatest possible combination of the spiritual forms of heat and light: energy or desire, and reason or vision. Fire destroys the solid form of nature, and those who have believed nature to be solid will find themselves in a lake of fire at the *Dies Irae.* But the imagination cannot be consumed by fire, for it is fire; the burning bush of God which never exhausts its material. It is this fire that "delights in its form."

The word "consummation," often applied to the apocalypse, refers both to the burning world and the sacred marriage. Paradise itself is a place of flaming fire, the fires being the "lustful" passions which there are fully gratified. They are also "thought-creating fires" because gratified desire produces reason. Eden is a fiery city, as is indicated in Ezekiel's speech to the Covering Cherub: "Thou hast been in Eden the garden of God . . . thou hast walked up and down in the midst of the stones of fire." Similarly the three whom Nebuchadnezzar put into a fiery furnace were seen to be walking unhurt in the fire with the Son of God.

Since the Fall, there has been a flaming sword over Paradise, and fire is now something to be approached with more circumspection. Orthodox theology tells us that in the eternal world the fires of hell have heat without light, and that heaven is a blaze of golden light, the question of heat being slurred over. Remembering that passion and desire are spiritual heat, such doctrines tell us symbolically that desires are hellish and that we shall be tortured forever for having them, whereas those who have emasculated their passions will be admitted to a heaven in which the kind of divine love they enjoy, while its exact nature is unknown, is certain to be something very, very pure. Like forest animals, the orthodox have a fascinated horror of fire and its torments, and when we come down to the skeptical obscurantism of the "new philosophy," "the element of fire is quite put out." What is coming is the union of heat and light, a marriage of heaven and hell. By "hell" Blake means an upsurge of desire and passion within the rising body so great that it will destroy the present starry heaven, and he calls it "hell" because that is what the orthodox call it. Here Blake's meaning has been misunderstood, and deserves more explanation.

Everything that furthers and increases the creative life is really good. The growth of creative energy is the tree of life which enables men to attain an eternal existence. Whatever is pleasing to society, whatever is cautious, prudent and undistinguished, or else vicious and cruel if society happens to be feeling that way, is morally good. The growth of morality is the tree of the knowledge of good and evil which leads to death. The former is the gospel; the latter the "law" under which all non-Christians, and most of the nominal Christians, live. Michael explains to Adam in *Paradise Lost* that it is the business of the law to discover sin rather than remove it. Moral good and moral evil do not represent any genuine opposition. The one wages wars and executes criminals; the other murders. The one exploits labor; the other robs. The one establishes marriage on the destruction of virginity; the other rapes. But they have a common enemy, the power of genius and prophecy. In terms of moral good it is not the murderer or the robber but the prophet who is really evil. Barabbas may be safely released, for it is impossible that his robberies can destroy the social structure of Pilate and Caiaphas; but there is deadly danger in Jesus and John the Baptist, who must be got rid of at all costs.

That is why no one can be saved by moral virtue. But it does not follow that Barabbas is in a higher imaginative state than Caiaphas. This takes us back by another road to our distinction of contrary and negation. The criminal is not the contrary but the negation of the morally good man; he breaks the law, but he has no gospel. And though the prophet is regarded by society as a devil or messenger from hell, he never practises the vice of "hindering another." There is much that is really good in moral good: the prophet is concerned only to disentangle it from the easy virtue of moral cowardice.

*The Marriage of Heaven and Hell,* therefore, has nothing to do with the simple inversion of moral good and evil which is known as sadism, and which forms an important aspect of Romantic culture. This is a traditional error in the interpretation of Blake, and one which ignores the fact that Blake attaches two meanings to the word "hell," one real and the other ironic. There is a real hell in the human mind, and it achieves the physical form of dungeons, whips, racks and all the miserable panoply of fear. Such a hell consolidates a moral virtue founded on terror with a moral evil founded on cruelty, and it exists because it is believed to be a part of "necessity." The more degenerate the society, the more obvious this alliance of moral good and evil against the power of genius becomes. Those who know better can see that, as evil is a negation, this hell would be, in the spiritual world, nothingness, a monstrous multiple of zero. No one could go on living in it after the Last Judgment, because no one can exist in a state of nonexistence, the post-apocalyptic hell of unending torment being, like the fallen sun, "a phantasy of evil Man." Whatever foreshadows the Last Judgment thus foreshadows the annihilation of hell, and of the believers in it who are negations, "the Elect from before the foundation of the world," and can have no existence after those foundations have disappeared. Hence for these "Elect" anything which makes persecution and oppression seem less "necessary," that is, any blow struck for human freedom, is their hell, and the announcement of a new hope, a new courage, a new faith and a new vision is, to them, "the voice of the devil." The darkness does not comprehend the light; evil spirits fade on the crowing of the cock, and from their point of view it is the cock that is the evil spirit, the herald of the light which afflicts them with the "frantic pain" of the spirit in the "Mad Song."

We have more definite evidence for the same point in *The Ghost of Abel,* which is addressed to Byron and is apparently conceived as an answer to that poet's *Cain.* Cain is provided by Byron with a great deal of imaginative vision.

He knows that the tyrant of the sky who demands docility is unworthy of worship, for if Adam had ignorance Jehovah had malice. He knows that his true enemy is death, and suspects that the flaming sword before Paradise has something to do with death. With the aid of Lucifer he journeys into previous worlds far older than Adam of "past leviathans" and a Golden Age of "intelligent, good, great, and glorious things," returning to the earth dizzy with a star-dazzled enlightenment. In the course of the journey Lucifer has dropped the suggestion that "it may be death leads to the highest knowledge," which links itself at once with Cain's own feeling that the understanding of death is his own ultimate victory—in other words, with the converse principle that the highest knowledge leads to death. It is from this that the state of mind develops which prompts him to murder Abel. Blake's conception of Byron's meaning is, apparently, that imaginative vision has something diabolic attached to it, and that the visionary is not only doomed to be an outcast and an exile, but that even crime may well be an inseparable part of a genius above the law, as illustrated in a murder which was the product of an intellectual awakening.

*The Ghost of Abel* makes the point that murder cannot be part of genius but is always part of morality, and that genius must break with virtue and vice alike. It is "bad" to commit a murder: granted, but it does not thereby become "good" to murder the murderer. That is the monotonous pendulum of revenge which goes on ticking all through history. Abel worshiped a "good" God who wanted sheep murdered; Cain in killing him was sacrificing to a "bad" God who wanted human beings murdered. But both were the same God, and that God Satan, who makes all his virtue out of necessity. Both Cain's murderousness and Abel's desire for revenge encourage this Satan to proclaim, in a parody of the Biblical account, that human blood is more acceptable to him than the blood of animals. The true God descends at once and sets a mark on Cain to prevent the meaningless counteraction of "bad" crime and "good" punishment from going any further.

All philosophies founded on sense experience are founded on a timid fear of expanding the powers of the mind, which uses the senses. All life lived on such principles takes caution and fear to be cardinal virtues. That is why "reason" in the bad sense is the same thing as morality. Here again we see that *The Marriage of Heaven and Hell* belongs in the tradition of great satire. *A Tale of a Tub* shows us how the official theologies of Christianity are all rationalizings directed to one end, the end of getting along with a fallen world, and of achieving as much Selfhood domination in it as possible. In other words, it makes the identification of reasoning and moral virtue complete. The next step is for Swift to add to this portrayal of the intellectual and moral degradation of man, a physical degradation. The body is the form of the soul, and the degraded soul is the filthy and nauseating aspect of the body. The Yahoo, therefore, is man

presented wholly in terms of his fall, and represents a conception of that fall
not greatly different from the one set forth in Blake.

Satire is an acid that corrodes everything it touches, and Blake saw in the
acid bath he gave his engravings a symbol of his approach:

> But first the notion that man has a body distinct from his soul is
> to be expunged; this I shall do by printing in the infernal method,
> by corrosives, which in Hell are salutary and medicinal, melting
> apparent surfaces away, and displaying the infinite which was hid.

This implies that condemnation is only part of the satirist's work: his attack
on the evil and foolish merely allows what he reveals to stand out in bolder relief.
The satirist who does nothing but watch people make fools of themselves is simply
pouring acid all over the plate, and achieves only a featureless disintegration.
But the great satirist is an apocalyptic visionary like every other great artist, if
only by implication, for his caricature leads us irresistibly away from the passive
assumption that the unorganized data of sense experience are reliable and consistent, and afford the only means of contact with reality. Satirists often give to
life a logical and self-consistent shift of perspective, showing mankind in a telescope
as wriggling Lilliputians, in a microscope as stinking Brobdingnagians, or through
the eyes of an ass, like Apuleius, or a drunk, like Petronius. In satire like this
the reality of sense experience turns out to be merely a series of customary associations. And in Rabelais, where huge creatures rear up and tear themselves out
of Paris and Touraine, bellowing for drink and women, combing cannon balls
out of their hair, eating six pilgrims in a salad, excreting like dinosaurs and
copulating like the ancient sons of God who made free with the daughters of
men, we come perhaps closest of all to what Blake meant by the resurrection
of the body. Rabelais' characters are what Blake called his "Giant forms," and
they are the horsemen who ride over the earth in the day of the trumpet and
alarm, where we, in our sublunary world, see nothing but anguish and death:

> The enemies, after that they were awaked, seeing on one side the
> fire in the camp, and on the other the inundation of the urinal deluge,
> could not tell what to say, nor what to think. Some said, that it
> was the end of the world, and the final judgment, which ought to
> be by fire.

*The Marriage of Heaven and Hell,* with its blistering ridicule of the wisdom
that dwells with prudence, with its rowdy guffaws at the doctrines of a tortur-
ing hell and a boring heaven which are taught by cowards to dupes, is perhaps
the epilogue to the golden age of English satire. It has been said that in Blake's
"To the Muses" the eighteenth century dies to music. The eighteenth century

was a little too healthy to expire in any such trifle, and perhaps it would be better to say that in *The Marriage of Heaven and Hell* the age of Swift and Sterne and Fielding and Hogarth plunges into a vigorous Beethovenish coda which, though organically related to what has gone before, contains much new material and is big with portents of the movements to follow.

# The Eternal Hell Revives

*David V. Erdman*

> *Drive your cart and your plow over the bones of the dead.*
> *The road of excess leads to the palace of wisdom. . . .*
> *Exuberance is Beauty.*
>
> — "Proverbs of Hell"

In *The French Revolution* we see what a deep and steady furrow Blake has determined to plow across the graveyard of old ideas and old allegiances. In *The Marriage of Heaven and Hell,* a collection of manifestos and proverbs and "Memorable Fancies" in parody of Swedenborg's "Memorable Relations," we see what a contrary and revolutionary step Blake has persuaded himself to take from an interest in the New Church to an enthusiasm for the new society. We see at the same time how useful Swedenborg's theosophical analytics are as something for Blake to transcend by contradiction, reading black for white. "Without Contraries," he now argues, there can be "no progression."

Blake's progression from Wilkite patriotism in the 1770s to humanitarian Christianity in the late 1780s to political radicalism in the 1790s is dramatic but hardly unique. It has a shadowy but definite parallel in the career of William Sharp, as we have seen. And doubtless Blake was not the only recipient of new light at the Swedenborgian General Conference of April 1789 who soon received a much brighter light from France. In the golden dawn of the Rights of Man many Christians felt that Christ's humanity was perhaps more important than his divinity. Consistent with Blake's endorsement of Fayette and Orleans and Bailly and other great men associated with the reduction of the Bastilles of repres-

From *Blake: Prophet against Empire.* © 1954, 1969 by Princeton University Press. Princeton University Press, 1969.

sion is his call to those who worship Christ to love him as the greatest *man* and to honor God's gifts in all men, "loving the greatest men best . . . for there is no other God."

Theological and political humanitarianism often went together—and with them moral emancipationism. While the French commons were interpreting their *cahiers,* the London theosophists were quarreling over the implications of Swedenborg's *Chaste Delights of Conjugal Love: after which follow the Pleasures of Insanity & Scortatory Love.* Some favored a doctrinal recognition of "the inborn *amor sexus"* as an irrepressible force, a question which takes on strongly political meaning for Blake and may have done so for some of the Swedenborgians. Those who went so far as to condone fornication and concubinage, however, were expelled. For all their talk about the Active Life, most readers of Swedenborg recoiled from naked Energy displayed and were morally and politically passive. They enjoyed Swedenborg's *Heaven and Hell and their Wonders as heard and seen by the Author* but did not seem to hear and see the wonders taking place in the world about them. On the second anniversary of Bastille Day the Church-and-King rioters in Birmingham understandably confused the Swedenborgian Temple of Joseph Proud with the Unitarian Chapel of Joseph Priestley and would have set fire to them both. Yet Proud—who would later fail to persuade Blake to join his London community—had already chosen the path of rituals, vestments, and other Ceremonies rather than the Active Life, and his assurances that the New Church was no threat to Church or King were as genuine as the guineas with which he accompanied them.

Blake continued to purchase and annotate new volumes of Swedenborg as the society issued them, for a year or so, but the tone of *The Marriage* and of his extant marginalia is that of satiric and doctrinal opposition. If Swedenborg had been able to read the Bible as "celestial arcana," Blake was now in the light of history learning to read it as "infernal." He had already rounded on the pious with a declaration that active evil is better than passive good. If that sounded like a proverb from Hell, he was now inspired by the French Revolution and Tom Paine to write down seventy more. "Prayers plow not! Praises reap not!" Swedenborg had conversed only "with Angels who are all religious, & conversed not with Devils who all hate religion"; his account of Hell was but hearsay.

Butter would not melt in the mouths of these religious Angels, but they were frightened "almost blue" by the new wisdom of Devils—and to such people all prophets seemed Devils, Isaiah and Ezekiel as well as Paine and Rousseau. One Angel is frightened terribly by his own analysis of the future yet cannot see Blake's. Another is violently upset at first by the Orleanist creed of Equality and is anxious about questions of law and order, as sworn to in the society. "Has not Jesus Christ given his sanction to the law of ten commandments?"

But this Angel finally accepts enlightenment, and embraces "the flames of fire" to be consumed and arise as Elijah. As a Prophet or Devil he becomes Blake's "particular friend," and they "often read the Bible together in its infernal or diabolical sense which the world shall have if they behave well." It is pleasant to hear once more the confident mockery of Quid and to learn that he enjoyed the company of a convert to his own corresponding society.

Blake's *Marriage of Heaven and Hell* mocks those who can accept a spiritual apocalypse but are terrified at a resurrection of the body of society itself. "Energy is the only life and is from the Body," announces the Devil, and it is "Eternal Delight" though the religious may call it Evil (pl. 4). The birth and resurrection of Christ are not the equal and opposite exhalations of the theosophists but progressive stages in the life of man. Blake rejects Swedenborg's "spiritual equilibrium" between good and evil for a theory of spiraling "Contraries" that will account for progress. "Attraction and Repulsion, Reason and Energy, Love and Hate, are necessary to Human existence" (pl. 3). Such *unnecessary* opposites as Bastilles and Moral Codes and the "omissions" due to poverty are merely hindrances that may be scattered abroad "to the four winds as a torn book, & none shall gather the leaves." They "spring from" the *necessary* Contraries but are not to be confused with them. Christ stamped the ten commandments to dust, and history will not return to them except perversely.

Blake is half in jest when he speaks of the "marriage" of Heaven and Hell, for Hell does not exist except as the negative way of looking at Energy, while the Heaven of things-as-they-are is really a delusion like the senile "innocence" of Har and Heva which springs from a denial of the true Heaven of progression. Blake's theory admits of a true or necessary Reason as "the bound or outward circumference of Energy" but leaves it no role in "life" except to be pushed about. Reason is the horizon kept constantly on the move by man's infinite desire. The moment it exerts a will of its own and attempts to restrain desire, it turns into that negative and unnecessary Reason which enforces obedience with dungeons, armies, and priestcraft and which Blake refers to as "the restrainer" which usurps the place of desire and "governs the unwilling." Tiriel was such a deity, and so is the dismal god of the Archbishop of Paris who can no longer restrain the millions from bursting the bars of Chaos. Blake will soon invent for this sterile god a comic name, Nobodaddy (old daddy Nobody), and an epic name, Urizen, signifying *your reason* not mine) and the limiting *horizon* (Greek ὁρίζειν, to bound). The poet's hostility toward this "Governor or Reason" is thoroughly republican or, to the modern mind, socialistic.

Blake's intransigence toward any marriage of convenience between Hell and Heaven appears further in an extended metaphor of conflict which he introduces with a play upon Rousseau's pronouncement that man is born free but is everywhere in chains:

> The Giants who formed this world . . . and now seem to live in
> it in chains are in truth, the causes of its life & the sources of all
> activity, but the chains are, the cunning of the weak and tame minds,
> which have power to resist energy. . . .
>
> Thus one portion of being, is the Prolific, the other, the Devour-
> ing: to the Devourer it seems as if the producer was in his chains,
> but it is not so, he only takes portions of existence and fancies
> that the whole.

There is a substratum of reference here to the economic struggle of producer and exploiter or producer and consumer, not without a Mandevillean echo.
This struggle is "eternal" in the sense that the producer and consumer even in
the false relationships of slavery and commerce are doing what must always be
done to sustain life. They are doing it the cheerless way, but even in the freedom
of a classless paradise there will always be work and always an audience for the
artist-workman, for "the Prolific would cease to be Prolific unless the Devourer
as a sea received the excess of his delights."

But Blake's more immediate focus is upon the politics of moral restraint,
and he is condemning the conservatism which seeks to confine the oppressed
to a passive acceptance of tyranny. "Religion is an endeavour to reconcile" the
"two classes of men" who "should be enemies," i.e., to unite the lion and its
prey. But "Jesus Christ did not wish to unite but to separate them, as in the
Parable of sheep and goats! & he says I came not to send Peace but a Sword."
The illusion that energy can be quietly repressed by celestial "wisdom" is ex-
ploded by the very fact of revolution. But the fear that revolution means the
cessation of all productive relations and of the very means of existence is equally
illusory, as Blake proceeds to demonstrate in his fourth "Memorable Fancy."

In this parable Blake and a conservative Angel who is alarmed at his radical
"career" undertake to show each other the post-revolutionary future from their
respective points of view. The Angel is unwilling to plunge with Blake into
the void of the coming century to see whether the Swedenborgian "providence
is here also," because what he sees ahead is a "monstrous serpent" with a forehead
colored "green & purple" like "a tygers." This is what the Revolution looks
like to a Tory, and it is symbolic of the fear of Hell which makes him restrain
desire. The monster that terrifies him boils up out of the nether deep beside
a "cataract of blood mixed with fire" in a manner that prefigures the birth of
Orc in *America* which terrifies the King of England. Blake's "friend the Angel"
is frightened away. But Blake stands his ground; and since he does not allow
himself to be imposed upon by the Angel's "metaphysics," he finds that he ends
up, not in the belly of a monster, but sitting peacefully "on a pleasant bank

beside a river by moonlight hearing a harper who sung to the harp, & his theme was, The man who never alters his opinion is like standing water, & breeds reptiles of the mind." The Angel is quite surprised to find that Blake has "escaped" alive. But it is only to the stagnant mind that the energy of revolution appears reptilian and sympathy with rebellion a career leading to a "hot burning dungeon . . . to all eternity."

Blake then "imposes upon" the Tory in his turn, showing this Guildenstern a vision of *his* future lot, assuming the Swedenborgian Hell to be true. The Tory's clinging to the status quo means that he accepts a phantasmal eternity of cannibalistic relations between Producers and Devourers. A person who assumes that people belong in chains and who scorns the multitude as swinish has nothing to look forward to but a loathly conflict of "monkeys, baboons, & all of that species chaind by the middle." The Devourers, politician-like, grin and kiss "with seeming fondness" the body of a victim they are devouring limb by limb. The implication seems to be that only those who cannot imagine progressive social change must view the Negations as eternal and assume that human relations will be forever those of joyless slavery.

In one of the dens of Blake's Bastille there is a prisoner of the shorn Samson type, with his "feet and hands cut off, and his eyes blinded," who is the victim of a similar illusion. Like the frightened Angel he believes that Destiny is really on the side of the tyrannic forces that imprison him: "fancy gave him to see an image of despair in his den, Eternally rushing round, like a man on his hands and knees . . . without rest." To minds so imposed upon by the terrors of the old order, the shining sun itself is "black." . . .

> The harvest shall flourish in wintry weather
> When two virginities meet together
>
> The King & the Priest must be tied in a tether
> Before two virgins can meet together
>
> . . .
>
> For on no other ground
> Can I sow my seed
> Without tearing up
> Some stinking weed
>
> —Notebook 106, 111

By the summer of 1792 it was plain that old Nobodaddy was not going to expire voluntarily. "Precisely while the Prussian batteries were playing their briskest at Longwi in the Northeast," says Carlyle, priest-benighted La Vendee in the Southwest was exploding *against* the Revolution—"a simple people, blown into flame and fury by theological and seignorial bellows!" In Paris the royalists grew bolder, the people more desperate, as invading armies approached. There would be no *wise* innocence and no peace, it seemed, until both king and priest were tethered with a shorter rope than the veto-suspended Constitution. Before France could hope to sow and harvest the wheat of Liberty, every stinking weed of the old system would have to be cleared away.

This is the language of some fragmentary verses in Blake's notebook. They lack the explicit historical allusions of *Fayette,* but we know from that ballad that Blake felt he could understand such summary wielding of the destructive sword against aristocrats and royalist priests as took place in the "September Massacres":

> But the bloodthirsty people across the water
> Will not submit to the gibbet & halter

In his published work of this period, Blake's allusions to counterrevolutionary threats, the people's patriot wrath, and the birth of the new republic in clouds of war are indirect, symbolic, and often blended with more direct allusions to the American Revolution. Yet a familiarity with the metaphors of *Fayette* and *The French Revolution* and the simplest reconstruction of the historical context will restore the contemporary allusions and implications. [Here,] we shall read three short and more or less cryptic poems against the background of the coming into being of the French Republic. The lyric "Argument" of *The Marriage of Heaven and Hell,* probably written in late 1790 or early 1791, depicts in Biblical imagery the meek driven to wrath; the psalmodic *Song of Liberty,* a later appendage to *The Marriage,* is an epithalamium of the new republic; and apocalyptic in its implications is the great revolutionary lyric, "The Tyger," written before *Fayette* in 1792 or early 1793.

The spirit of *The Marriage* is one of sunny confidence, but the "Argument," bracketed in an ominous refrain, suggests the darker context of war and rumors of war:

> Rintrah roars & shakes his fires in the burdend air;
> Hungry clouds swag on the deep.

Blake had used a similar image in "Gwin":

> The Heav'ns are shook with roaring war,
> And dust ascends the skies!

In both cases the theme is counterrevolution. The swagging (lowering) clouds are doubtless war clouds hungry for blood. The roaring and the deep suggest the stormy roar and wintry seas of counterrevolution in *Fayette*. "Rintrah" plays no further part after this roaring in the prologue and so must remain unidentified, though in later poems he will emerge as Wrath and sometimes as William Pitt, British leader of the crusade against France. Even in 1790 Pitt pushed a chance of war with Spain; in the spring of 1791 he threatened the use of force against Russian expansion and was dissuaded partly (according to Coleridge) by English popular opposition.

In his *French Revolution* Blake had imagined the commons planting "beauty in the desart craving abyss" and had hoped that the priest would "No more in deadly black" compel the millions to "howl in law blasted wastes." In the first prose page of *The Marriage* he announces "the return of Adam into Paradise." The "Argument" begins with a reacapitulation of the hopeful first stage of the revolution (when, according to *The French Revolution,* the meek peasant came out of the feudal shadow of death and was free to "woo in pleasant gardens" and plant a fair harvest):

> Once meek, and in a perilous path,
> The just man kept his course along
> The vale of death.
> [Now] Roses are planted where thorns grow,
> And on the barren heath
> Sing the honey bees.

As oppression gave way to peace, "the perilous path was planted" and man was reborn in Eden. But then came the conspiracy of aristocrats and priests, as the concluding stanzas indicate. The "villain" or "sneaking serpent," i.e., the priest or any pious hypocrite opposing freedom (compare the "crawling villain" in *America*), agitated for counterrevolution and plotted to drive the righteous into the wilderness once more.

As early as the publication of Burke's *Reflections* in October 1790, the ideological issue was joined. During the next two years, as Blake worked over the revision and amplification of his "infernal" vision of history, the clouds enlarged and darkened in both France and England.

Two components of the anti-Jacobin spirit in the summer of 1792 are relevant. On the borders of France the army of the French Princes, mounted on English horses, was mustering under the July Manifesto of the Duke of Brunswick in which their imperial and royal majesties of Austria and Prussia threatened to exterminate "the town of Paris and all its inhabitants without distinction" unless they would submit at once to their king. "Deserts are preferable to people in revolt," the leagued kings declared. In London the émigré priests, conspicuous in their robes as symbols of the ancient heavens, went about with increasing confidence, as English politicians anxious to secure the mark of anti-Jacobinism made a great show of sympathy in their support.

The future had promised to be "a pleasant bank beside a river by moonlight." But now, realizing Blake's "Argument,"

> the villain left the paths of ease,
> To walk in perilous paths, and drive
> The just man into barren climes.

Leaving their prerevolutionary indolence, the priests were inciting kings to take the path of war and counterrevolution:

> Now the sneaking serpent walks
> In mild humility.
> And the just man rages in the wilds
> Where lions roam.

While French priests were walking about London like upright serpents, the French people were "raging . . . in forests" to confront the lions of the royal armies. "The priest promotes war," Blake wrote in his notebook. The threat to turn flourishing cities into deserts was compelling patriots to become warlike men.

The *Song of Liberty* at the other end of *The Marriage* celebrates the casting out of French monarchy and the rout, less than two months after his roaring manifesto, of Brunswick's starry hosts, who were forced into a dismal and muddy retreat from Valmy even as the new Republic was being announced in Paris, at the end of September. The climactic cry, *"Empire is no more!"* is applied retrospectively to America and prophetically to the Spanish and Papal empires, to the commercial imperialism of the London slave trade, and to London's god, Urizen. But the inspiring fact is that Republicanism in France, "the son of fire in his eastern cloud" born in "the American meadows," has come through fire-baptism, has braved the war clouds "written with curses" (an allusion perhaps to the manifesto), and has simultaneously dethroned French monarchy and hurled back the lion of Austria and the wolf of Prussia from the wintry door. A "Chorus" admonishes royalist priests whose "accepted brethren" are tyrants to take heed and cease cursing the sons of freedom ("sons of joy"): "For every thing that lives is Holy."

The British tyrant, scarcely recovered from the military and moral reverses of the American War (recapitulated in verse 15), is most vividly reminded of those reverses by the September events in France. Glancing "his beamy eyelids over the deep," he is filled with "dark dismay" at what he sees across the Channel where "the morning plumes her golden breast." There is prophecy of the demise of his own Empire in the proclamation of a Republic so close to London. Blake makes the prophecy more explicit in a declaration at the end of *America,* of which this *Song of Liberty* is a preliminary sketch (or later summary). . . .

A drawing that precedes *A Song of Liberty,* worked up subsequently into a striking color print, depicts the archetypal emperor, Nebuchadnezzar of Babylon, fallen and crawling naked and woebegone in desert exile. In France a king has been dethroned, and the true nature of monarchy as a "bound and outward circumference" too narrow for the infinite desires of humanity, is now revealed. Every "jealous king" who limits the horizons of others, every "Urizen" who drives the just into barren climes, does so because he understands deserts better than people and because his own vision is so limited that a correct portrait shows him on hands and knees in that pre-human state described hypothetically by Rousseau: "his long nails [are] crooked talons; . . . his whole body, like that of a bear, [is] covered with hair." If man ever lived as such an animal, Rousseau observed, "the nature and limits of his ideas" would be indicated by "the fact that he walked upon all fours, with his look . . . confined to a *horizon* of a few paces."

Blake's identification of fallen Reason with Nebuchadnezzar is a striking instance of his creative and complexly ironic use of traditional material. The pictorial details, the body, the talon-nails, the impossibly hairy back and thighs, derive from his admired Mortimer's drawing of *Nebuchadnezzar recovering his Reason,* the 1781 etching of which was doubtless in Blake's print collection. And the association of this bestial man with Reason is suggested by Mortimer's title. But Blake, shifting the subject to Nebuchadnezzar's fall, proceeds to draw the ironic emblem of Reason *losing* his reason.

The creeping Urizen is supplied with a long soliloquy in a passage in Night V of *The Four Zoas* which is worth taking up here for the light it casts back upon *The Marriage* and *A Song of Liberty* — and "The Tyger." The fatal error of the jealous king is that his fixing of the horizon ultimately limits himself more than it does the energy of the people. Royalty can keep its crimson robes, Orleans warned, only if it stops trying to measure for each man "the circle that he shall run." Soliloquizing as he crawls in the den or narrow circle of his own ideas, the fallen Urizen of Night V laments too late his imperial mistakes: his choice of war instead of peace, his failure to accept the opportunity to be an enlightened despot when the "mild & holy voice" of divine freedom said, "O light, spring up & shine" and "gave to me a silver scepter & crownd me with a golden crown" to "Go forth & guide" the people. "I went not forth," he laments; "I hid myself in black clouds of my wrath[;] I called the stars around my feet in the night of councils dark" (64:21–26). Thus George assembled his council in 1774; thus Louis prepared his "starry hosts" in 1789 and let the spark of humanity in his bosom be "quench'd in clouds" by "the Nobles of France, and dark mists." Each time, in the event, at Yorktown and again at Valmy, "The stars threw down their spears & fled naked away. We fell." Too late Urizen is sorry he refused the use of his "Steeds of Light" (64:27; 65:6).

The language of this soliloquy is doubly revealing. On the level of practice it is clear that "The stars threw down their spears" means: the armies of counter-revolution were defeated. On the level of theory it is clear that Reason, when it refuses to assist but attempts to hinder Energy, is overthrown. Denied the peaceful accommodation of the Steeds of Light, the just man seizes the Tigers of Wrath. Vetoed by a stubborn monarch, the French people became, as the London *Times* of January 7, 1792, put it, "loose from all restraints, and, in many instances, more ferocious than wolves and tigers." As Blake put it in *Fayette,* the French grew bloodthirsty and would "not submit to the gibbet & halter."

If we take the tiger and horse as symbols of untamed Energy and domesticated Reason, then it is obvious which of these contraries is the more vital in days of revolution. In Hell it is proverbial that "the tygers of wrath are wiser than the horses of instruction," and the devil Isaiah assures Blake "that the voice of honest indignation is the voice of God." Yet when revolt tears up one social contract, it must establish a new "free" one, based on an active marriage of Reason and Energy. The revolution "stamps the stony law to dust" as the last act of wrath against reason, but in so doing it looses "the eternal horses from the dens of night, crying *Empire is no more! and now the lion & wolf shall cease.*" This cry at the end of *A Song of Liberty* and at the climax of the Declaration of Independence as rendered in *America* is virtually a declaration that the age of reason is the true Jerusalem. Voltaire and Rousseau are still the guiding fire and cloud. The era of the beasts of prey gives way to the era of the untethered horses of intellect, who are of the order of Swift's Houyhnhnms. On this closing page of *A Song of Liberty* the text is illuminated with dashing and prancing horses. One bears a rider, but with no reins or saddle. We see no more of lion, wolf, or tiger.

Nevertheless, according to the Devil at least, the roaring of lions and the howling of wolves "are portions of eternity," even though "too great for the eye of man" and perhaps too great for the mind of man. Blake's famous Song of Experience, "The Tyger," raises the cosmic question: How can the tiger of experience and the lamb of innocence be grasped as the contraries of a single "fearful symmetry"? The answer, suggested in question form, is that the very process of the creation of the tiger brings about the condition of freedom in which his enemies (his prey) become his friends, as angels become devils in *The Marriage.* The tiger in Blake's illustration of this poem is notoriously lacking in ferocity, and critics have sometimes concluded that Blake was unable to "seize the fire" required to draw a fearful tiger. He could at least have tried, but he is showing us the final tiger, who has accomplished his mission, has even, perhaps, attained a state of organized innocence as have the adjacent lions and tigers of "The Little Girl Lost" and "The Little Girl Found" who demonstrate that "wolvish howl" and "lions' growl" and "tygers wild" are not to be feared.

The creative blacksmith who seizes the molten stuff of terror and shapes it into living form on the cosmic anvil must employ dread power as well as daring and art, but the dread, Blake hopes, will be sufficient unto the day. The climax of the forging is a mighty hammering which drives out the impurities in a shower of sparks, like the falling stars children call angels' tears. At this point in "The Tyger," Blake employs the symbols which in his political writing signify the day of repentance when the king's "starry hosts" shall "throw down . . . sword and musket," the nobles and priests "shall weep, and put off . . . war," and the "wild raging millions, that wander in forests" shall become "mild peaceable nations" walking "in bliss."

> When the stars threw down their spears
> And water'd heaven with their tears:
> Did he smile his work to see?
> Did he who made the Lamb make thee?

The creator must have smiled at Yorktown and at Valmy, not because his people were warlike, but because they seemed ready to coexist with the Lamb, the wrath of the Tiger having done its work. The question, "Did he smile his work to see?" is perhaps as rhetorical as the corresponding query of Orleans: "And can Nobles be bound when the people are free, or God weep when his children are happy?"

This is not to imply that "The Tyger" is a political allegory but to point out that the fire in which the tiger is forged can be recognized as a general form of the fires that "inwrap the earthly globe" in the first year of the French Republic. The tiger burning in the forests of the night is a vision in the same mind that saw in Necker a hind threatening to burn down "the ancient forests of chivalry," that saw portions of eternity wherever men were struggling to be free—"a Serpent in Canada . . . In Mexico an Eagle, and a Lion in Peru; . . . a Whale in the South-sea"—and that would see, in another year, wrathful lions and bloodthirsty tigers in "the vineyards of red France."

# Dialectic of *The Marriage of Heaven and Hell*

*Harold Bloom*

*The Marriage of Heaven and Hell* assaults what Blake termed a "cloven fiction" between empirical and a priori procedure in argument. In content, the *Marriage* compounds ethical and theological "contraries"; in form it mocks the categorical techniques that seek to make the contraries appear as "negations." The unity of the *Marriage* is in itself dialectical, and cannot be grasped except by the mind in motion, moving between the Blakean contraries of discursive irony and mythical visualization.

Apocalypse is dialectical in the *Marriage,* as much so as in Shelley's *Prometheus* or the poems by Yeats written out of *A Vision,* or in Blake's own Night the Ninth of *The Four Zoas.* The great difficulty of dialectical apocalypse is that it has got to present itself as prophetic irony, in which the abyss between aspiration and institution is *both* anticipated and denounced. The specific difficulty in reading *The Marriage of Heaven and Hell* is to mark the limits of its irony: where does Blake speak straight? In Blake, rhetoric subsumes dialectic, and usurps its place of privilege. But the process of usurpation is not clear, though this is no flaw in Blake as poet and polemicist. *The Marriage of Heaven and Hell* is a miniature "anatomy," in Northrop Frye's recently formulated sense of the term, and reserves to itself the anatomy's peculiar right to mingle satire with vision, furious laughter with the tonal complexity involved in any projection of the four or more last things.

I suggest that we need to distinguish between the *Marriage* as in itself dialectical and the dialectic it attempts to present. The same distinction, rigorously

From *The Ringers in the Tower.* © 1971 by the University of Chicago. University of Chicago Press, 1971.

set forth, would clear away much of Yeats's deliberate perverseness in *A Vision,* and might help in the comprehension of the epics of Blake. The *schemata* of those epics, though dialectical, are yet systematic; the local life in them maddeningly (but gratefully) defies the system. The *schemata,* as Frye in particular has extracted them, present *the* dialectics, early and late, of Blake; the texture, of *Jerusalem* especially, is so dialectical as to put *the* dialectics in doubt. Not that Blake mocks himself; only that he mocks the Corporeal Understanding (including his own) and refuses unto death to cease setting traps for it. There is, in consequence, a true way of reading Blake, put forward by Blake himself, a first-class critic of his own works. But this is a true way which, as Kafka once remarked of true ways in general, is like a rope stretched several inches above the ground, put there not to be walked upon but to be tripped over.

I shall attempt to reduce the *Marriage* to Blake's own overt dialectic in what follows, but because it is not primarily a discursive work I make this attempt in a spirit of tentativeness, respecting its innate trickery.

The poem that opens the *Marriage* as "argument" has not been much admired, nor much understood. Rintrah, the angry man in Blake's pantheon, rears and shakes his fires in the burdened air; clouds, hungry with menace, swag on the deep. The poem is a prelude, establishing the tone of prophetic fury that is to run beneath the *Marriage;* the indignation of Rintrah presages the turning over of a cycle.

The poem itself has the cyclic irony of *The Mental Traveller.* The "just man" or "Devil" now rages in the wilds as outcast, having been driven out of "perilous paths" by the "villain" or "Angel." This reversal is simple enough, if it is true reversal, which it is not. The initial complication is provided by the sixth to ninth lines of the poem:

> Roses are planted where thorns grow,
> And on the barren heath
> Sing the honey bees.

*Grow,* not *grew; sing,* not *sang.* We are already involved in the contraries. Cliff is opposed to river, tomb to spring, bleached bones to the red clay of Adam (literal Hebrew meaning). The turning of this cycle converts the meek just man into the prophetic rager, the easeful villain into the serpent sneaking along in mild humility. The triple repetition of "perilous path" compounds the complication. First the just man keeps the perilous path as he moves toward death. But *"then* the perilous path was planted . . . / *Till* the villain left the path of ease, / To walk in perilous paths."

We grasp the point by embracing both contraries, not by reconciling them. There is progression here, but only in the ironic sense of cycle. The path, the way of generation that can only lead to death, is always being planted, the just man is always being driven out; the villain is always usurping the path of life-in-death. When the just man returns from being a voice in the wilderness, he drives the villain back into the nonexistence of "paths of ease." But "just man" and "villain" are very nearly broken down as categories here; the equivocal "Devil" and "Angel" begin to loom as the *Marriage's* contraries. The advent of the villain upon the perilous path marks the beginning of a new "heaven," a "mild humility" of angelic restraint. So Blake leaves his argument and plunges into his satiric nuptial song:

> As a new heaven is begun and it is now thirty-three years since its advent, the Eternal Hell revives.

Swedenborg, writing in his *True Christian Religion,* had placed the Last Judgment in the spiritual world in 1757, the year of Blake's birth. In 1758 Swedenborg published *his* vision of judgment, *Heaven and Hell.* Now, writing in 1790, at the Christological age of thirty-three, Blake celebrates in himself the reviving of the Eternal Hell, the voice of desire and rebellion crying aloud in desert places against the institution of a new divine restraint, albeit that of the visionary Swedenborg, himself a Devil rolled round by cycle into Angelic category.

Before the *Marriage* moves into diabolical gear, Blake states the law of his dialectic:

> Without Contraries is no progression. Attraction and Repulsion,
> Reason and Energy, Love and Hate, are necessary to Human existence.

The key here is *Human,* which is both descriptive and honorific. This is a dialectic without transcendence, in which heaven and hell are to be married but without becoming altogether one flesh or one family. By the "marriage" of contraries Blake means only that we are to cease valuing one contrary above the other in any way. Echoes of Isaiah 34 and 35 crowd through the *Marriage,* and a specific reference to those chapters is given here by Blake. Reading Isaiah in its infernal sense, as he read *Paradise Lost,* Blake can acknowledge its apocalypse as his own. As the imaginative hell revives, the heaven of restraint comes down.

> And all the host of heaven shall be dissolved, and the heavens shall
> be rolled together as a scroll: and all their host shall fall down.
> (Isa. 34:4)

The Promethean release that has come to Blake with his full maturity is related to the titanic fury of French revolution and English unrest that is directly contemporary with the *Marriage.* The Revolution is the active springing from Energy, called Evil by the "religious," who assign it to Hell. Frye has stated the central idea of the *Marriage* as being the analogy of this unrest to the biblical time of troubles that precedes the end of the world. The *Marriage* thus enters the category not of "How long O Lord?" prophecy but of the "turn now" injunction based on Hillel's famous question, "If not now, when?" So that its dialectic must cease to be purely descriptive and cyclic, which is to say, must cease to be merely dialectic. Apocalypse does not argue, and hardly needs to convince. The verse of the Negro spiritual carries in a kernel the authoritative message of apocalypse, taking place between the sardonic warning and the dreaded effect: "You will shout when it hits you, yes indeed."

Therefore, the contraries, when next stated in the famous "Voice of the Devil" passage, have ceased strictly to be contraries. Blake's lower or earthly paradise, Beulah Land, is a state of being or place where contraries are equally true, but the *Marriage* is written out of the state of Generation, our world in its everyday aspect, where progression is necessary. Christian dualism is therefore a negation, hindrance, not action, and is cast out beyond the balance of contraries. Blake does not build truth by dialectic, being neither a rational mystic like Plato nor a mystic rationalist like Hegel. Nothing eternal abides behind forms for Blake; he seeks reality in appearances, though he rejects appearance as it is perceived by the lowest-common-denominator kind of observer. Between the cloven fiction of St. Paul's mind-body split and the emotionalism of the celebrator of a state of nature exists the complex apocalyptic humanism of the *Marriage,* denying metaphysics, accepting the hard given of this world, but only insofar as this appearance is altogether human.

Here it has been too easy to mistake Blake—for Nietzsche, for D. H. Lawrence, for Yeats, for whatever heroic vitalist you happen most to admire. The *Marriage* preaches the risen body breaking bounds, exploding upward into psychic abundance. But here Blake is as earnest as Lawrence, and will not tolerate the vision of recurrence, as Nietzsche and Yeats do. The altogether human escapes cycle, evades irony, cannot be categorized discursively. But Blake is unlike Lawrence, even where they touch. The Angel teaches light without heat, the vitalist—or Devil—heat without light; Blake wants both, hence the marriage of contraries. The paradise of Milton needs the heat of hell; the earth of Lawrence needs the light of Eden, the rational fire of intellect and creation. Rhetoric now carries the *Marriage* through its implicit irony; Blake speaks straight for once before subjecting *Paradise Lost* to the play of dialectic:

> Energy is the only life, and is from the Body; and Reason is the bound
> or outward circumference of Energy.
>     Energy is Eternal Delight.

This does not mean that Reason, the bound, is Eternal Torment; it does mean that Reason's story would hold that unbounded Energy *is* such torment. Hence the *Marriage's* curious double account of fall and negative creation, whether of hell or heaven:

> For this history has been adopted by both parties.
> It indeed appear'd to Reason as if Desire was cast out; but the Devil's account is, that the Messiah fell, and formed a heaven of what he stole from the Abyss.

In crude terms, the problem is where the stuff of life comes from; where does Reason, divinity of the "Angels," obtain the substance that it binds and orders, the energy that it restrains? By stealing it from the *Urgrund* of the abyss, is Blake's diabolic answer. We are almost in the scheme of *The Four Zoas:* the Messiah *fell,* stole the stuff of creativity, and formed "heaven." One contrary is here as true as another: this history has been adopted by both parties. One party, come again to dominance among us, now condemns Blake as a persuasive misreader of *Paradise Lost.* When, in another turn of the critical wheel, we go back to reading *Paradise Lost* in its infernal or poetic sense, as Blake, Shelley, and a host of nineteenth-century poets and scholars did, we will have to condemn a generation of critical dogmatists for not having understood the place of dialectic in literary analysis.

The "Memorable Fancies," brilliant exercises in satire and humanism, form the bulk of the *Marriage,* and tend to evade Blake's own dialectic, being, as they are, assaults, furious and funny, on Angelic culpability. The dialectic of the *Marriage* receives its definitive statement once more in the work, in the opposition of the Prolific and the Devouring. If one grasps that complex passage, one is fortified to move frontally against the most formidable and properly most famous section of the *Marriage*, the "Proverbs of Hell," where dialectic and rhetoric come together combatively in what could be judged the most brilliant aphorisms written in English, seventy gnomic reflections and admonitions on the theme of diabolic wisdom.

The Titanic myth, the story of "the Antediluvians who are our Energies," is always present in Blake, though frequently concealed in some contrapuntal fiction. In the *Marriage* the myth is overt and "Messiah *or* Satan" is identified with these Giant Forms. The *or* establishes again the marriage of contraries. The Giant Forms, huge ids, or Orcs, to use Blake's vocabulary, are bound down by the cunning of weak and tame minds:

> Thus one portion of being is the Prolific, the other the Devouring: to the Devourer it seems as if the producer was in his chains; but it is not so, he only takes portions of existence and fancies that the whole.

> But the Prolific would cease to be Prolific unless the Devourer,
> as a sea, received the excess of his delights.

This terrifying vision of the economy of existence is mitigated by its irony, and yet moves into mystery in its final statement. Reason and the senses do not bound our energies; Eternal Delight, the primal Exuberance that is Beauty, exists beyond the bounds. Blake is not predicating an unconscious mind, for that would be only a widening of the circumference of the bound. The Freudian hypothesis of the unconscious would have represented for Blake what it does to the phenomenologists—a premature cessation of mental activity, a refusal to analyze all of the given. But Blake more than anticipates Husserl here; he gives a definitive statement of the phenomenology of existence, the ceaseless dialectic of daily appearance. Yeats, in *A Vision,* proudly asserted his refusal to be logical, lest he be trapped by his own dialectic. He had never believed with Hegel, he wrote, that the spring vegetables were refuted because they were over. In this he was caught up in Blake's spirit, in the vision of existential contraries. The Angel or Devourer takes all the negative force of Blake's rhetoric, but dialectically he is a necessity. The Prolific will not be confined, but it needs constraint, it thirsts for battle. The Devourer is a sea, a moat imprisoning the creator, who would otherwise be choked in the excess of his own delight. Without the hard given (a wall is as good a symbol as a moat) we do not engage in the mutable struggle. This war cry passes into the most defiant sentences in the *Marriage:*

> Some will say: "Is not God alone the Prolific?" I answer: "God only
> Acts and Is, in existing beings or Men."
> These two classes of men are always upon earth, and they should
> be enemies: whoever tries to reconcile them seeks to destroy existence.
> Religion is an endeavour to reconcile the two.

The nontheism of Blake is never more clearly stated than here, and yet is still being misread by many. If God only acts *and is* in Men, then *God* has become an unnecessary hypothesis, having no abstract being beyond our powers of visualization and confrontation. To destroy enmity between Prolific and Devourer would destroy existence, such destruction being religion's attempt to inflict upon us the greatest poverty of not living in a physical world. Blake's dialectical stance, with its apotheosis of the physical and its rejection of the merely natural, is most frequently misunderstood at just this point. Against the supernaturalist, Blake asserts the reality of the body as being all of the soul that the five senses can perceive. Against the naturalist, he asserts the unreality of the merely given body as against the imaginative body, rising through an increase in sensual fulfillment into a realization of its unfallen potential.

Religion seeks to end the warfare of contraries because it claims to know a reality *beyond* existence; Blake wants the warfare to continue because he seeks a reality *within* existence. Milton's heaven knows no strife, and therefore no progression, and is to Blake—hell.

We can see Blake's interplay between dialectic and espousing one pole of the dialectic most vividly in the "Proverbs of Hell," where the revelation of the laws of process and a fierce antinomianism are frequently interleaved:

> The road of excess leads to the palace of wisdom. (3)
> Prudence is a rich, ugly old maid courted by Incapacity. (4)
> He who desires but acts not, breeds pestilence. (5)
> If the fool were to persist in his folly he would become wise. (18)
> The Tygers of wrath are wiser than the horses of instruction.
>     (44)
> You never know what is enough unless you know what is more
>     than enough. (46)
> Exuberance is Beauty. (64)
> Sooner murder an infant in its cradle than nurse unacted desires.
>     (67)
> Where man is not, nature is barren. (68)

Each of these proverbs depends for its true meaning on a dialectic definition of desire and act, though rhetorically the meaning is overtly antinomian. Desire is positive; it leads to an action which is not the hindrance of another. Act is positive and is virtue; Blake, commenting on Lavater, defines its contrary as "accident":

> Accident is the omission of act in self & the hindering of act in another;
> This is Vice, but all Act is Virtue. To hinder another is not an act;
> it is the contrary; it is a restraint on action both in ourselves & in
> the person hinder'd, for he who hinders another omits his own duty
> at the same time.

The road of excess has therefore nothing to do with sadism or self-destruction, but is the way to that all, less than which cannot satisfy us. Incapacity, which courts Prudence, is a mode of hindrance. Desire which does not lead to action is also "accident," vice, and is self-destructive. The fool persisting in his folly at least acts; ceasing, he is merely foolish, and falls into self-negation. Instruction may draw you on, but wrath will take you sooner into wisdom, for wrath embodies desire. The boundary of desire you learn only by moving beyond, and the furious energy of this liberation is definitive of beauty. To *nurse* an unacted desire *is* to murder an infant in its cradle; overt murder is at least more positive.

Last, take man and his struggle of contraries out of nature, and you are left with the barren, with the same dull round over again, the merely cyclic movement, if such it can be termed, of negations.

The last plate of the *Marriage* has upon it the figure of King Nebuchadnezzar eating grass like an ox, in a hideous emblem of the return to a state of nature. Nebuchadnezzar haunted Blake; Blake meant him to haunt us. When you forget the contrary of vision, when waking you reject the lessons of the night, then you suffer the negation: you feed like beasts upon the grass.

# The Body of Imagination

*Thomas R. Frosch*

The dictum in *The Marriage of Heaven and Hell*, that all forms of energy are from the body is relevant at this point, as is the strange Memorable Fancy in which Blake describes the printing house of Hell:

> I was in a Printing house in Hell & saw the method in which knowledge is transmitted from generation to generation.
>
> In the first chamber was a Dragon-Man, clearing away the rubbish from a caves mouth; within, a number of Dragons were hollowing the cave,
>
> In the second chamber was a Viper folding round the rock & the cave, and others adorning it with gold silver and precious stones.
>
> In the third chamber was an Eagle with wings and feathers of air, he caused the inside of the cave to be infinite, around were numbers of Eagle like men, who built palaces in the immense cliffs.
>
> In the fourth chamber were Lions of flaming fire raging around & melting the metals into living fluids.
>
> In the fifth chamber were Unnam'd forms, which cast the metals into the expanse.
>
> There they were receiv'd by Men who occupied the sixth chamber, and took the forms of books & were arranged in libraries.

The process begins with the sexual widening of the doors of perception by the monsters of energy, who renew the senses by sweeping them clean of habitual and institutionalized restrictions. At this excess, the Viper attempts to bind the sexual body, to keep it within the natural context and, by producing all the

From *The Awakening of Albion.* © 1974 by Cornell University. Cornell University Press, 1974.

allurements of a natural existence, to celebrate the sufficiency of sex as an end in itself. In opposition, the Eagle of imagination, the "portion of Genius" of the "Proverbs of Hell," rises from the feeling of freedom and unrestricted possibility that results from the cleansing in the first chamber. Next, the Lions of prophetic wrath, in accord with the teachings of Ezekiel in the earlier banquet scene, resist present ease and gratification and melt down the non-human beauties of nature into the primal substance of a new being. The formless fluids are committed to a chamber of the new and the unknown, whose workers, themselves nameless, or unformed, cast them into the human world, where, received by men, as the Prolific imagination by the Devouring rational consciousness, they appear as books.

In this account the artistic process begins with an upsurge of sexual fulfill-ment and culminates, by means of an enlarged awareness of bodily pleasure, in a poem. The process can be read, loosely, as analogous to the making of Eden, in which the responsibility of man for his life is a kind of poetic work and the final products are no longer books but realized human lives. In Blake sexual desire is ultimately a desire for a non-natural paradise; and through the artistic work of Los, who combines the functions of Eagle, Lion, and Unnamed Form, the progression from Generation to Upper Beulah to Eden is gradually accomplished. What the progression depends upon is a rise from genitality, which cannot be called a sublimation because it is a rise from genital satisfaction and even seems to be inspired by it. Lawrence, I think, is particularly close to Blake when he describes in *Fantasia of the Unconscious* a sense of renewal following the individual "commingling of sex," a new energy and enthusiasm that stimulates us to "the great purpose of manhood, a passionate unison in actively making a world. This is a real commingling of many." We should bear in mind, however, that the naturalistic Lawrence would probably have approved of Blake's description of Edenic sexuality not as a literal potentiality of the senses but as an allegory of collective work, thereby reducing the new heaven and earth of *Jerusalem* to the redeemed nature of *Milton*.

It seems that the total human activity in any State of Being is simultaneous-ly a sexual and a creative activity; the themes of sensory improvement, produc-tion and reproduction, and the relationship of male and female always refer to both. The distinction between art and sexuality is maintained, however, until the final transformation, when both, as we know them, drop out; in their place is the commingling of the risen body, an interplay of faculties with each other and with the total environment they delineate, in which imagination and sexual love reassume their identity, just as soul and body or perception and creation. Then the word "body" once again signifies the "real man" and the "whole man," as well as "all men"; and the fiery lineaments of a finally gratified desire are perceived in the tactility of a complete human speech.

# Polar Being

*Martin K. Nurmi*

During the time Blake was producing *Songs of Experience,* he was also writing and etching a work of a very different kind, *The Marriage of Heaven and Hell,* begun, as indicated in a chronological reference in the text, in 1790 but not completed until 1792 or 1793. It is a strange work, a kind of philosophical manifesto, partly in satiric form, affirming the polar nature of being and the need for a change in man's perception so that this polar nature can be recognized. The immediate object of the work, arising from its satiric theme, was to expose and reject the normative moral categories of Good and Evil of orthodox religion by showing that Good and Evil are merely abstractions, distortions of the vital "contraries" that inform all being and that must be allowed to function without restraint in human life. Good and Evil as ordinarily conceived deny each other and are hence what Blake later calls "negations." In *The Marriage,* he explains "what the religious call Good & Evil" really are: "Good is the passive that obeys Reason[.] Evil is the active springing from Energy. Good is Heaven. Evil is Hell." And he "marries" them—or rather reunites them—as reason and energy in this philosophical manifesto. But for satirical purposes, he retains the orthodox terms through much of the work and seems to be turning ordinary morality upside down as he exalts energy as Hell. Some readers, including Swinburne, have accordingly misunderstood his purpose and have taken him to be a satanist.

*The Marriage* is the second statement in his philosophical countersystem, the tractates being the first. *Songs of Innocence and of Experience* could also be included as part of this in the sense that two sets of songs develop a concept in moral philosophy also involving a kind of contrariety, which, however, is somewhat different from that in *The Marriage.* Blake's manifesto in *The Marriage*

From *William Blake.* © 1975 by Martin K. Nurmi. Hutchinson and Company, 1975.

is, as I suggested the tractates were, satiric in form. It seems appropriate for a countersystem to be partly satiric, making error clearer by exposing it as ridiculous. The immediate object of satire in *The Marriage* is Emmanuel Swedenborg, though the whole rationalist religious complex of which Swedenborg is a part is the real target.

As was mentioned earlier, Blake and Catherine had for a brief time become officially Swedenborgians, even signing a set of resolutions at a conference of the New Church in London in 1789. But Blake quickly became disillusioned and was sharply critical of Swedenborg's apparent extrapolation of earthly predestinarianism into the next world in a way that would seem to turn heaven partly at least into a replica of earth—and would certainly seem to deny the possibility of the apocalypse which Blake worked to bring about, through art, all his life. Blake was probably attracted to Swedenborg because Swedenborg, a scientist, had experienced visions and had based a religion on them. But as he went farther into Swedenborg's works, after finding much to admire in those of 1784 and 1788, he came to feel that the scientist turned visionary was, after all, one of the religious reasoners: that his conversion to vision was incomplete and his visions contaminated. Later on he was more charitable toward Swedenborg, calling him a "Samson shorn by the Churches," or a "divine teacher" who has "done much good, and will do much good." But even then he seldom failed to add that Swedenborg was nevertheless "wrong in endeavouring to explain to the *rational* faculty what the reason cannot comprehend." In *The Marriage* he showed little charity. Where Swedenborg had described in elaborate detail in his *Heaven and Hell* (1784) how the "hells," of which there were not one but many, were kept separate from heaven and ruled by angels, Blake marries them. And where Swedenborg has said "Without equilibrium there is neither action nor reaction," Blake, rejecting equilibrium as dead, static, explicitly opposes to it the main principle of *The Marriage*: "Without Contraries is no progression. Attraction and Repulsion, Reason and Energy, Love and Hate, are necessary to Human existence." Formally, *The Marriage* proceeds by alternating sections of theoretical exposition and "memorable fancies." The latter are parodies of Swedenborg's "memorable relations" among the angels, the accounts, written in very matter-of-fact language, of angelic conversations.

Swedenborg is not mentioned in the poetic account given in a letter that Blake wrote Flaxman in 1800, speaking of his "lot in Heaven" and of the spiritual events that were important in it. That part of the poem is worth quoting fully because it contains elements important to the background of *The Marriage* to which I shall have occasion to refer later. After expressing gratitude to Flaxman for his friends in his "lot on Earth," Blake tells of his lot in heaven:

Now my lot in the Heavens is this, Milton lov'd me in childhood
    & shew'd me his face.
Ezra came with Isaiah the Prophet, but Shakespeare in riper
    years gave me his hand;
Paracelsus & Behmen appear'd to me, terrors appear'd in the
    Heavens above
And in Hell beneath, & a mighty & awful change threatened
    the Earth.
The American war began. All its dark horrors passed before
    my face
Across the Atlantic to France. Then the French Revolution
    commenc'd in thick clouds,
And My Angels have told me that seeing such visions I could
    not subsist on the Earth,
But by my conjunction with Flaxman, who knows to forgive
    Nervous Fear.

Blake was in Felpham at this time, grateful to Flaxman for his "present Happiness" in his cottage, building a new life under the patronage of William Hayley, painting miniatures and doing other work that he hoped would provide more earthly happiness than he had enjoyed. For the moment, he seemed a prophet of apocalyptic revolution gone underground out of a "nervous fear" that was to be justified in the trial for treason at the end of the Felpham sojourn. But this came later. A decade earlier, in *The Marriage* and in his prophetic accounts of the revolutions in France and America, he was more forthright, responding to visions of heaven and hell that were more powerful than those to be found in Swedenborg's memorable relations among the angels. And he was formulating metaphysical conceptions to match, in which Swedenborg was of little help.

    Among the men to appear to him, as noted in the poem, were Paracelsus (Theophrastus Bombastus von Hohenheim, the German physician and alchemist) and "Behmen" (Jacob Boehme, the "Teutonic Theosophist" popularized in England by William Law). In *The Marriage* Blake explicitly devalues Swedenborg in comparison with these men, by a factor of ten thousand to one: "Any man of mechanical talents may from the writings of Paracelsus or Jacob Behmen, produce ten thousand volumes of equal value with Swedenborg's." It is rather hard to find any very direct influences on Blake from Paracelsus—and tracing influences in Blake is a most uncertain business at best because everything he borrows becomes very much his own. But there do seem to be some echoes of Boehme in Blake's development of his idea of the contraries. Some of the vigour of his rejection of Swedenborg may have come about because Swedenborg's religious ideas seemed to him so thin compared with those of Boehme.

But Blake hardly needed Boehme as a source for his idea of the contraries. Heraclitus' idea that being comes from strife or subsists in strife was a commonplace that appeared everywhere, in a variety of places in poetry ranging from Spenser to Pope. The Pythagoreans founded a whole system of the universe on polarities; and Bayle's dictionary made available extended accounts of polar metaphysics in discussing Manicheanism. Even the great — or, as Blake would have it, "the little" — Bacon took basic oppositions into account as aspects of nature, calling them "Transcendentals or Adventitious Conditions of Essences" (*De Dignitate*). Blake had only to adapt to his own purposes ideas that were readily available.

Moreover, since he was in *The Marriage* interested in reunifying human life, which he saw as being split by rationalized religion, into normative moral categories of Good and Evil and since his imagination was a visionary one that had to develop a total order of imagery in mythic form, he was perfectly capable of re-inventing this idea himself. Polarities, opposites, dualisms are simply fundamental experiences in human life and nature — in sexuality, in bilateral bodies, in root ideas like hot and cold, and so on — and mythic thinking deeply reflects these. So, in their own way, do the ordinary concepts of Good and Evil. But to Blake, dividing existence into Good and Evil implied a religion based on abstract reason rather than a direct relationship with God, a morality of negative commandments which could be utilized to suppress the impulse to know God, and it could generate or at least support institutions like monarchies. The typical manifestation in man's life in the world was "corporeal war," in which one part of the human race tried to destroy another part. Good and Evil were religio-moral ideas which in political action led inevitably to oppression and destruction. And in religion they implied a god to match, whom Blake early called "Nobo-daddy" (i.e., nobody's father) and later identified as Urizen (from, possibly, material existence: "your-eyes-on," from "horizon," or from "*your*-reason," which is to say, not mine).

Later on he would make allowance for evil, of a kind, as having a real existence. But in *The Marriage* he wanted, as did his disciple Yeats, to get beyond good and evil. He wanted not only to redeem the contraries from their distorted state as Good and Evil in materialistic, rationalized religion but also to show the way to a knowledge of the real ground in which the contraries in human life would be seen as creative rather than destructive; and that ground was the imagination which connected man with God.

Pope invokes the strife of opposites in the *Essay on Man* as inevitable though not perhaps desirable:

> Better for Us, perhaps, it might appear,
> Were there all harmony, all virtue here;

That never air or ocean felt the wind;
That never passion discomposed the mind.
But All subsists by elemental strife;
And Passions are the elements of Life.
The gen'ral Order, since the whole began,
Is kept in Nature, and is kept in Man.

(1:165–72)

The ground in which opposites operate and are harmonized is nature or man himself. And the opposites are merely accepted as necessary but uncomfortable facts of life. Pope's harmony is more an equilibrium than a harmony. In his idea of the contraries, as we have seen, Blake is not satisfied with equilibrium. His contraries interact with vigour. But more important, his contraries are not harmonized in some external order; "the gen'ral Order" is not "kept" by anything, certainly not in nature or fallen man who believes in the efficacy of nature as providing a cosmic order. For Blake the "order" is the interaction of the contraries in the cosmic imagination of which man is a part. "Reason and Energy" in The Marriage—which might be roughly equated with contraction, or form, and expansion, or genius—are essential to human life in Blake's special sense of the word "human"—a state in which man's imagination has been liberated from the "mind-forg'd manacles" of false philosophies (of the kind which Pope subscribes to) and man has realized the essential divinity of his own nature. In this state, the contraries, though opposed to each other, are not negations bent on each other's destruction and hence do not need to be harmonized by some external agency. If, for purposes of conceptual discrimination, we say that they function in some kind of unifying "field" which could perhaps be thought of as a universe in which they coexist in their creative conflict, that field is the totality of being in the cosmic imagination.

Negations like Good and Evil attempt to hinder and even destroy. Blake's contraries do not. They pull in different directions, vigorously so in the "mental war" which at the apocalypse will replace [the] corporeal; but they work, as it were, with mutual respect and love. They have an inherent unity in being what they are, and the identity of each implies the existence of the other, somewhat as male implies female, and vice versa. Unity for Blake "is as much in a Part as in the Whole" in art and in everything else.

Since, moreover, all of being is organized as contraries, Blake's contraries do not disappear in some sort of higher synthesis. Nor is the "progression" in which they function one in which they change their identities, as the opposites do in Hegelian dialectic. The progression in human life to which they are essential is the progression of continued creativity; and if it goes anywhere it goes toward fuller realization of the divinity that is in humanity through continued fruits of a life lived with the divine imagination, rather than nature, as the ground of being.

Blake's doctrine of the contraries is quite clearly not merely Heraclitean or anything else. It is his own. To be sure, Heraclitus, like Blake, criticized a spokesman of the religious establishment of his time, Homer, for not allowing room for the contraries in his scheme of being. Blake's objective is to put forth an idea which, if taken seriously, would help bring about the apocalypse, a gigantic change of man's mind which would show that "mental things are alone real" and that real freedom in its most comprehensive sense was not only possible but necessary. *The Marriage* is an apocalyptic document. One of its tasks was to expound the doctrine of contraries, which we have just been considering. The other was to show by what means the real nature of being could be known: in other words, to use philosophical jargon, what kind of epistemology was necessary to know real existence. I touched earlier on his expanded sense-perception which included the potential for synoptic fourfold vision and other lesser degrees of vision. This expanded sense-perception, which involves as much imagination as possible, now becomes another main theme in *The Marriage,* taking up most of its middle section.

I have dwelt this long on the main ideas of *The Marriage* partly because they are important for later works but also partly to avoid long digressions in the discussion of the work itself, which is a fascinating mixture of satire, apocalyptic doctrine, philosophical doctrine, and as Northrop Frye has remarked, "rowdy guffaws."

*The Marriage,* comprising twenty-seven plates, is arranged structurally into an opening Argument and then into six alternating expository sections each followed by a "memorable fancy." Added to it is a *"Song of Liberty"* that applies politically the ideas developed in *The Marriage.* Thematically considered, the work divides into three main sections, the first dealing with the idea of contraries (to plate 6), the second with expanded sense-perception (from plate 6 through 14), and a third returning to the contraries again in the light of thematic development of the idea of sense-perception (plate 15 through 24).

The title-page shows a number of embracing figures flying upward from an abyss bounded on the left by the fires of "Hell" and on the right by the clouds of "Heaven" through a nether sky to a walk among trees. And the Argument suggests that some kind of change is imminent in its opening lines,

> Rintrah roars & shakes his fires in the burdend air;
> Hungry clouds swag on the deep[.]

Blake could not expect his reader to know who Rintrah is, for this character makes his first appearance here. But the revolutionary mood is clear enough—

and, as Erdman suggests, Rintrah may be an ironic version of Pitt, and the fires and clouds of the opening lines were appearing in France. The Argument proper gives an account of what happened to the "just man" in a little fable:

> Once meek, and in a perilous path,
> The just man kept his course along
> The vale of death.
> Roses are planted where thorns grow.
> And on the barren heath
> Sing the honey bees.

But then the perilous path itself was domesticated, "planted," and Adam, the natural man was created: "on the bleached bones / Red clay brought forth," Adam's name literally meaning red clay. The Fall has occurred in the entrenchment of material creation, and the path of the just man (which in Proverbs 4:18 "is as the shining light" though here it was "perilous" to those who do not understand the contraries in human life) has been usurped by the "villain," and humility has been left to the serpent while the just man "rages in the wilds." The repetition of the opening lines at the end of the argument suggests that this situation will soon change. Rintrah may express God's anger in Isaiah 34 and hint at the change that follows it in Isaiah 35. Blake gives the scriptural references in the next section of *The Marriage*.

The first expository section, on plate 3, states the theme of the contraries already referred to and also introduces the satire on Swedenborg and the new heaven of his New Church. "Heaven" is here, as it usually is in Blake, ironic. Swedenborg's new heaven was begun thirty-three years before, a time period which makes its beginning identical with Blake's own birth and also suggests that, since Christ was thirty-three at the crucifixion and resurrection, the new heaven was brought about by his death. This is reinforced by Swedenborg's being "the Angel sitting at the tomb; his writings are the linen clothes folded up." Swedenborg's theology has only to do with the dead Christ worshipped by material religion. But as "new heaven is begun . . . the Eternal Hell revives," being revived not only through the negations of Good and Evil necessary to a religion postulating a heaven of smug righteousness but also revived in the ironic sense in which Blake uses "Hell" in *The Marriage*—the repressed energy that is excluded from the realm of being by conceptions such as heaven, whether new or old. Then Blake states the main theme of this section:

> Without Contraries is no progression. Attraction and Repulsion,
> Reason and Energy, Love and Hate, are necessary to Human existence.
> From these contraries spring what the religious call Good & Evil.

> Good is the passive that obeys Reason[.] Evil is the active springing
> from Energy. Good is Heaven. Evil is Hell.

The next section, "The Voice of the Devil," is not called a "memorable
fancy," but it works like one, introducing a concrete dramatic element to follow
the dogmatic opening section. The devil's statements have often been taken as
those of Blake himself. To be sure, Blake, as one of the active contraries among
mankind, would certainly incline to be "of the devil's party," as he said Milton
was. And we would not go too far astray to let the devil speak for Blake—not
as a Satan but as what "the religious" think of the devil as being. But as a par-
tisan spokesman for energy, the devil is not much interested in the marriage
of reason and energy. Accordingly, when as a contradiction to one of the errors
that "All bibles or sacred codes" have been guilty of, he asserts that "Man has
no Body distinct from his Soul for that calld Body is a portion of the Soul discernd
by the five Senses, the chief inlets of Soul in this age," the devil is speaking the
truth—but not quite the whole truth: he avoids mention of the interaction of
body and soul required by Blake's theory. Likewise, when he says "Energy is
the only life and is from the Body [admitting, perhaps, that he should have
acknowledged body in the previous statement] and Reason is the bound or outward circumference of Energy," he is again overstating.

The second expository section gives a penetrating psychological account of
the authoritarian personality: "Those who restrain desire, do so because theirs
is weak enough to be restrained; and the restrainer or reason usurps its place
& governs the unwilling." And he goes on to apply it to the growth of
authoritarian religion, saying that a long institutionalized system of repression
all but destroys desire altogether. Even Milton was not free of restraint when
writing of "Angels and God," but he could write "at liberty when of Devils
& Hell, . . . because he was a true Poet and of the Devils party without
knowing it."

Blake is quoted from the next section more often than from any other place,
for we now move to a view of Hell, where we first see a mighty devil etching
a pair of lines drawn from Chatterton on the side of the cliff:

> How do you know but ev'ry Bird that cuts the airy way,
> Is an immense world of delight, clos'd by your senses five?

This applies the idea from the first tractate of *There Is No Natural Religion* that
"From a perception of only 3 senses or 3 elements none could deduce a fourth
or fifth." The narrator collects seventy "Proverbs of Hell," thinking "that as
the sayings used in a nation, mark its character, so the Proverbs of Hell, show
the nature of Infernal wisdom better than any description of buildings or
garments." These proverbs invite comparison with those in the Old Testament,

and may be intended to form part of the "Bible of Hell" announced at the end of *The Marriage,* developing some of the devil's codes as "Proverbs" develops moral virtue. In general, the proverbs exalt the active over the passive ("Expect poison from the standing water") and also exalt excess ("The road of excess leads to the palace of wisdom") as opposed to restraint and moderation, which are adventitious limits. In counselling "excess," therefore, the proverbs adopt the rhetoric and categories of "the religious," for infernal wisdom sees everything as good, even the pride of the peacock, the lust of the goat, the wrath of the lion, and the nakedness of woman, all of which come from God. "Prudence," says one of the funnier proverbs, "is a rich ugly old maid courted by Incapacity" (no. 4). One of Blake's infernal proverbs has passed into pretty common usage: "The tygers of wrath are wiser than the horses of instruction" (no. 44). If, as the proverb says, "Exuberance is Beauty," the proverbs are beautiful indeed.

In the third expository section that follows, Blake takes up the theme of perception again, giving his adaptation of a fairly popular account of the rise of religions that appears in the work of Colin Maclaurin, the interpreter of Newton; Richard Payne Knight's *A Discourse on the Worship of Priapus . . .*; in Coleridge; and in Shelley. In Blake's succinct version of the process, the "ancient Poets animated all sensible objects with Gods or Geniuses" giving them the names and properties of nature, cities, and nations and of "whatever their enlarged & numerous senses could perceive"; then a "system was formed, which some took advantage of & enslav'd the vulgar" by abstracting the "mental deities from their objects" and making them real and mysterious, thus creating "Priesthood"; the next step was that they "pronounced that the Gods had ordered such things"; thus, the account concludes, "men forgot that All deities reside in the human breast." What starts out as the imaginative exaltation of natural objects is abstracted from objects, made a mystery requiring priestly interpreters, and finally turned into laws. In his annotations to Reynolds' discourse, Blake objected to the same sort of thing in Reynolds' making a general pattern into a norm from which every deviation is a "deformity." Since Blake often rejected external nature as non-existent, the importance he attached to the objects of nature in this passage may seem inconsistent, but it really is not. He is wholly consistent in saying that perception cannot be considered apart from an object, or at least discrete percepts cannot. Doing so leads to chaos: "Deduct from a rose its redness, from a lilly its whiteness from a diamond its hardness from a spunge its softness from an oak its heighth from a daisy its lowness & rectify every thing in Nature as the Philosophers do & then we shall return to Chaos & God will be compelld to be Excentric if he Creates O happy Philosopher." "The substance," he says, "gives tincture to the accident & makes it physiognomic."

The "memorable fancy" that follows parodies Swedenborg's blandly reported conversations with the angels. Blake has two of his favourite prophets, Ezekiel and Isaiah, in for dinner and asks them how they could be so sure that God spoke to them. Isaiah replied that he "saw no God, nor heard any, in a finite organical perception" but saw the infinite in everything and was "perswaded, & remain confirm'd; that the voice of honest indignation is the voice of God," and so wrote. Ezekiel gives an account of the poetic genius as the source of all perception. After dinner the narrator asks about lost works of both, but learns there are none; he also inquires about their extreme behavior, and is told that they had to behave that way and not care for the consequences. Ezekiel said he went barefoot for three years for the same reason as "our friend Diogenes the Grecian." In *An Island in the Moon*, Blake, it will be recalled, cast himself as Quid the Cynic, a modern Diogenes.

Plate 14, illustrated by a cadaverous recumbent body over which hovers a vigorous figure coming out of fire, brings the section on sense-perception to a climax, in the prophecy announced here that the apocalypse is at hand. The narrator exuberantly commands the "covering cherub" guarding the tree of life to leave, and "when he does, the whole creation will be consumed, and appear infinite, and holy whereas it now appears finite & corrupt." This will come about by the "improvement of sensual enjoyment" and the cleansing of perception, and these will be possible when the narrator—and here the *persona* clearly becomes Blake—has expunged the Cartesian notion that the body is distinct from the soul, which he will do by "printing in the infernal method," by the "corrosives" of philosophical criticism and satire in the etched form of his illuminated books.

The previous plate with its prophecy and reference to printing leads to the remarkable "memorable fancy" of the printing house in hell, which is Blake's version of the allegory of the cave. This is a rich section not easily summarized, but in general it develops both the idea of expanded sense-perception and the contraries together, in moving through five chambers into a sixth. In the first, sensual enjoyment and perception are cleared; in the second, a serpent (of form) folds himself around the rock to contain, in the third chamber, the interior imaginative expansion which occurs within the containing form; in the fourth chamber raging lions of fire melt metals, which are "cast" in the fifth "into the expanse" of imaginative form and received, in the sixth chamber, as books which are then arranged in libraries. Among other things, this section gives a visionary account of Blake's aesthetics. In the popular mind, visions are usually confused with hallucinations, and Blake was forever being asked silly questions like "where" did he see his visions, to which he on at least one occasion replied by tapping his forehead. The printing house in hell shows the process of expansion from within to the infinite, in an inversion of the Newtonian space of the corporeal world, an "opening of a centre," as Blake calls it elsewhere, that occurs inside not merely a rock but a rock around which is coiled a viper to make the space doubly constricted. But the imaginative expansion which occurs within the enclosed space that is hollowed out of the rock is by no means formless. The "unnamed forms" that cast the molten metals into the expanse in the fifth chamber are unnamed because they are imaginative forms for which ordinary names do not apply; but they are not for that reason vague or blurry. Blake's ideal in pictorial art is "the wiry bounding line" without which art becomes chaos, and visionary art more than any other had to be minutely discriminated:

> The great and golden rule of art, as well as of life, is this: That the more distinct, sharp, and wirey the bounding line, the more perfect the work of art; and the less keen and sharp, the greater is the evidence of weak imitation, plagiarism, and bungling. . . . Leave out this l[i]ne and you leave out life itself; all is chaos again, and the line of the almighty must be drawn out upon it before man or beast can exist.

The fifth expository section attacks the monistic idea that denies any kind of duality and develops the doctrine of the contraries in dividing being into "the Prolific," which is active, and "the Devouring," which is passive. The Devouring half of existence thinks it is in power: "to the devourer it seems as if the producer was in his chains, but it is not so, he only takes portions of existence and fancies that the whole." Both are necessary, and both must retain their identities: "These two classes of men are always upon earth, & they should be enemies; whoever tries to reconcile them seeks to destroy existence." Blake's doctrine wants to "marry" the two but not to destroy their individuality and synthesize them. Religion, he says, wants to do this and hence seeks to destroy existence: "Religion is an endeavour to reconcile the two."

The fourth "memorable fancy" is the boisterous satiric climax of *The Marriage,* for Swedenborg in this section is due for devastating and rough treatment indeed. It is an altogether astonishing performance as some extremely complex ideas are expressed in a scene of robust, and sometimes gruesome, humor. This section is based on the prospects of two "eternal lots": that envisaged for the narrator by the pious Swedenborgian angel and that envisaged for the angel by the narrator. The first is a descent into a hell as seen by the angel, and the second is a brief space odyssey into empty abstract space, a sort of cosmic balloon flight, with Swedenborg's volumes literally as ballast.

The angel is horrified at the ideas presented in *The Marriage* thus far and warns the narrator that he is preparing himself for a "hot burning dungeon," whereupon the narrator suggests that they show each other their eternal lots. The angel takes him through a stable (of "the horses of instruction") and a church into the church vault and down a winding cavern to a nether void, where they finally sit in the roots of an oak, the angel being suspended upside down in a fungus. The view of the abyss which emerges by degrees from the smoke is a parody of a Swedenborgian view of hell. But suddenly there appears a monstrous serpent with streaks of green and purple "like those on a tygers forehead." It comes "to the east, distant about three degrees"—which is to say from Paris, which as Blake knew from his engravings of geographical books, was three degrees in longitude from London—and the angel sees it as Leviathan and departs in terror. The whole scene, being a projection of the angel's "metaphysics," changes to a peaceful one with the sound of a harper when the angel leaves. The angel's view of the narrator's eternal lot miscarried in the appearance of the revolutionary tiger-like creature from the east. For this lot, far from being eternal, was very much subject to change. The harper sings a song on the theme of one of the proverbs of hell, "The man who never alters his opinion is like standing water, & breeds reptiles of the mind," like the one just seen.

The narrator finds the angel again and proposes to show the angel his lot. The angel laughs but is seized by force in the balloon ascent through a cosmic scheme (that may have come from Boehme) to an abstract void, where they see the same stable and church and altar with a bible, which, now opened, shows a deep pit. They descend into it, the narrator driving the angel before him, and enter one of seven brick houses ("the seven churches of Asia"). The humor now turns gruesome in the spectacle of "a number of monkeys, baboons, & all of that species chaind by the middle, grinning and snatching at one another, but witheld by the shortness of their chains." But some were able to reach others, and "then the weak were caught by the strong and with a grinning aspect, first coupled with & then devoured, by plucking off first one limb and then another till the body was left a helpless trunk. this after grinning & kissing it with seeming fondness they devourd too." Returning, the narrator brings a skeleton, which in the mill "was Aristotles Analytics." The angel tries to shame the narrator, and he in turn replies that it is a waste of time to "converse with you whose works are only Analytics."

In the following expository section, Swedenborg is formally read out of the company of visionaries—if that was necessary after his space trip. And he is identified as a writer of "analytics": "Thus Swedenborgs writings are a recapitulation of all superficial opinions, and an analysis of the more sublime, but no further."

The last "memorable fancy," and the end of *The Marriage* proper, first presents a debate between an angel and devil, which the devil begins by announcing Blake's religion of man and God. The angel turns blue with horror but mastering his feelings turns yellow and at last "pink and smiling," as he replies with the idea that God is one, visible in Christ, and that Christ sanctioned the ten commandments, all other men being "fools, sinners, & nothings." The devil shows then that Christ himself broke all the commandments, but that "Jesus was all virtue, and acted from impulse, not from rules." At this, the angel and devil embrace and emerge as Elijah. The contraries are now married, and the angel-devil has become the narrator's friend. They read the bible in its "infernal" (visionary) sense together, and the narrator (Blake) announces his "Bible of Hell: which the world shall have whether they will or no." The whole work ends with the maxim: "One Law for the Lion & Ox is Oppression," not quite another proverb of hell but rather the necessary postulate for freedom within which the contraries can work.

Appended to *The Marriage* is *A Song of Liberty,* in twenty numbered statements with an exultant shout that "EMPIRE IS NO MORE!" and a "chorus" celebrating the holiness of life. This song furnishes a bridge between *The Marriage* and *America: A Prophecy,* making an apocalyptic application of the general doctrine of *The Marriage* in the political context of *America,* with some elements added.

Swedenborg may have been the proximate object of the satire in *The Marriage,* and the bouncing around he gets in it certainly provides most of the fun. But Blake's varied exposition of the contraries which furnish being with its essential vitality and his idea of the expanded sense-perception necessary to perceive—and hence to know, since for Blake knowledge is "immediate by sense"—makes *The Marriage* much more than satire. He will later make modifications in his idea of the contraries, making the pink and smiling angelic hinderers of positive act genuinely satanic; but the basic ontological doctrine of a polar being continues in his later work.

# The Problem of Dualism

*Leopold Damrosch, Jr.*

No saying of Blake's is more famous than "Without Contraries is no progression." Yet none is more problematic. It should be noted that he never repeated the statement in those terms, and found it far from easy to integrate a true dialectic of contraries in his later myth. To some extent, in fact, he tacitly repudiated the earlier doctrine, since he constantly strove to tame, limit, or expel some part of the contraries by reducing them to "negations," just as the unpleasant aspects of the fallen body were dismissed as "Non-Entity." But the ideal of the contraries remained very real to him, and the continuing publication of the *Songs of Innocence and of Experience* as "Shewing the Two Contrary States of the Human Soul" indicates its importance. Once again, I propose to establish an intellectual context that will show not only what Blake seems to mean, but also why he finds it so hard to mean what he wants.

To judge from passing references to Blake's contraries, one would think they represented nothing more than a claim that the world is full of a number of things and that by opposing each other, as many of them do, they contribute to a larger harmony. In these terms we are presented with something like Heraclitus' tension between opposites, the bow and the lyre. And it would be easy to invoke modern theories that see in the bipolarity of symbolic structures an inherent tendency of the mind. Ideas like these do seem to have inspired Blake at the time of *The Marriage of Heaven and Hell:* "Attraction and Repulsion, Reason and Energy, Love and Hate, are necessary to Human existence." But as I believe Blake saw with increasing clarity, such a statement, for all its fearlessness, is really no advance at all over the complacent Augustan notion of *concordia discors.*

From *Symbol and Truth in Blake's Myth.* © 1980 by Princeton University Press.

> But ALL subsists by elemental strife;
> And Passions are the elements of Life.
>
> (Pope, *Essay on Man*, 1:169–170)

In the Augustan tradition the strife of opposites always implies a damping down of energy in mutual accommodation. As Denham sternly describes the struggle between kings and people in Norman times, "one excess / Made both, by striving to be greater, less." In *The Marriage of Heaven and Hell* Blake confidently proclaimed the road of excess; in his later works the concept received a thorough reexamination. Surely, as Shelley said, the drama of contraries must not lead to "a catastrophe so feeble as that of reconciling the Champion with the Oppressor of mankind." In the end Blake would hold that error precipitates the victory of truth by taking a visible and therefore vulnerable form, the temporary triumph of Satan and Rahab. It ceases to be a question, in any simple sense, of a marriage of heaven and hell. And it would be hard to prove that at any time Blake was really comfortable with a marriage of contraries in the Heraclitean or Augustan sense.

It was a commonplace of "optimistic" explanations of evil that a successful picture needs shade as well as light:

> Here in full Light the russet Plains extend;
> There wrapt in Clouds the blueish Hills ascend.
>
> (Pope, *Windsor Forest*, 23–24)

And the goal of such oppositions was harmony: "All Discord, Harmony not understood." The later Blake explicitly rejects this aesthetic conception of opposition and harmony, just as he rejects the painterly aesthetics that it evokes as metaphor:

> The Sons of Albion are Twelve: The Sons of Jerusalem Sixteen
> I tell how Albions Sons by Harmonies of Concords & Discords
> Opposed to Melody, and by Lights & Shades, opposed to Outline
> And by Abstraction opposed to the Visions of Imagination
> By cruel Laws divided Sixteen into Twelve Divisions
> How Hyle roofd Los in Albions Cliffs.
>
> (*Jerusalem*, 74:23–28)

So much for *concordia discors* and lights and shades; they are instruments of "Hyle," matter and the fallen affections, and they imprison the visionary Los who sees outline and hears melody. When confronted with polarities Blake always tends to exalt one and repel or even exterminate the other.

Why then, does Blake deal with contraries at all? The reason is not that reality presents itself as a harmony of opposites, but rather that an inescapable experience of pain and struggle is fundamental to any achievement. Blake's Eden, in contrast with conventional images of heaven, is founded on this fundamental insight. So although Blake is constantly tempted to reject one half of any contrary pair, he is aware that to do so would be to falsify the truth as he perceives it. The contraries are a problem, not an answer. What has been said of Gnosticism could be applied word for word to Blake's myth:

> If the Gnostics propounded a dualist image of the world, it was not because their temperament predisposed them to see a contrary opposed to every entity, but because in the face of the omnipresent and tormenting evidence of evil, it was necessary to oppose something to it. But their goal was clearly to transcend this antimony, which only reflects the division and ripping apart that are characteristic of this world.
>
> (Lacarrière, *Les Gnostiques*)

Blake's immediate master in this area was Jacob Boehme, who believed that his theology could answer the kinds of questions raised here. Rather than absolving the remote Unknown God, as the Gnostics did, of responsibility for the bungled universe of an inferior demiurge, Boehme sought to identify the contraries with the very nature of God in the symbolism of fire as heat and light, "wrath" and "meekness," which Blake echoes with the terms "wrath" and "pity": "To cast Luvah into the Wrath, and Albion into the Pity / In the Two Contraries of Humanity & in the Four Regions" (*Jerusalem*, 65:3–4). At the time of *The Marriage of Heaven and Hell* Blake was clearly fascinated by Boehme's solution, which is closely reflected in his account of the Prolific and the Devouring, and in the statement that the Messiah "formed a heaven of what he stole from the Abyss." The "Eternal Death, or Devouring" is another name in Boehme's writings for the *Ungrund* or *Nichts,* the abyss that is beyond being "on the other side of good and evil, of Yes and No, of freedom and desire." But Boehme's doctrine requires that God be transcendent and unknowable, manifested only as his activity emerges into the world of active contraries from the mysterious abyss where desire is not. Moreover, the abyss is represented as a "dark world" of grief and horror, postulated as the necessary contrary of light and joy rather than as a positive value in itself. As Raine remarks, Blake ascribes "delight" to the devils in hell whom Boehme and Swedenborg saw as tormented and insane. But in his later works he seems no longer satisfied with the idea of a dark "abyss" either as the source of energy and delight (as with the devils in *The Marriage*) or, in Boehme's terms, as the fixed *contrarium* against which life and light can define themselves. Boehme developed his doctrine to explain how a good God can permit evil, showing that evil is the wrath that is the other face of meekness. In developing the idea of Urizen as demiurge, . . . Blake abandons Boehme for something much closer to the Gnostic position.

"To grasp evil in the Divine Being itself as the wrath of God," Hegel writes, "that is the supreme effort, the severest strain, of which figurative thought, wrestling with its own limitations, is capable, an effort which, since it is devoid of the notion [*Begriff*], remains a fruitless struggle." Hegel would say that Blake's myth is entrapped by its "figurative" conceptions, and would regret that Blake never elaborated the tantalizing suggestion of "progression" in "Without Contraries is no progression." It is tempting to understand Blake's aphorism as pointing to a Hegelian *Aufhebung,* the dialectic that simultaneously annuls each stage and raises it to a higher one. But the developed Blakean myth has no place for the upward spiral that absorbs each preceding stage, emphasizing instead that the spectral or Satanic must be expelled utterly. And in taking this position Blake tacitly recognizes the weakness of "progression," which is no easier to make sense of in Hegelian "concept" than it is in figurative form. As Taylor says, "The problem cannot be solved by a victory of one side over the other, by a simple undoing of separation in a spirit of unity; rather the two sides must be brought somehow to unity while each requirement is integrally satisfied. This is the task—perhaps an impossible one—which Hegel's mature system is meant to encompass."

Another way of describing Blake's position is to say, drawing on our discussion [elsewhere], that he will not admit the necessary role of the "other." He wants contraries but not otherness. Hence his account of the Negation is peculiarly tortuous and fraught with ambiguity. In Hegel it is axiomatic that "opposites negate each other, and since within everything that exists there is opposition, we can also say that within everything there is negativity." "Ich bin der Geist, der stets verneint!" says Goethe's Mephistopheles: "I am the spirit that continually negates." But Blake comes to see negation not as the interplay of opposites, but rather as a principle that stands *outside of* the contraries and is the spectral "false Body" that must be "put off & annihilated alway":

> There is a Negation, & there is a Contrary
> The Negation must be destroyed to redeem the Contraries
> The Negation is the Spectre; the Reasoning Power in Man
> This is a false Body: an Incrustation over my Immortal
> Spirit; a Selfhood, which must be put off & annihilated alway.
>
> (*Milton* 40:32–36)

The force of "alway" is to suggest that annihilation must be ever renewed, so that in fact the negation cannot be decisively abolished. But we are also told that the productive interaction of the contraries is distinct from negation. Blake's meaning is that reason cannot tolerate contraries but always strives to negate them, whereas spiritual vision rejoices in them. It is therefore possible to assert that the entire structure of *Milton* is built upon contraries. But I would argue that these interrelated pairs—time and space, male and female, time and eternity, lark and thyme—are not actually contraries at all, but opposed or reversed aspects of sameness.

In *Jerusalem* Blake states that contraries are made by the Sons of Albion, and that "From them they make an Abstract, which is a Negation." Contraries and negations alike are expressions of fallen existence, and call for radical redefinition in Eden or Eternity. Meanwhile the Negation may have an ironically active role, as in *Milton* when Satan's mills are needed to grind the apocalyptic harvest. And Satan is a son of Los just as Rintrah and Palamabron are. But when Los is restored to his eternal condition as Urthona, Satan will not be reabsorbed into him; as the great design on plate 10 shows, Rintrah and Palamabron preserve the Boehmian categories of wrath and pity, while Satan—who represents what Boehme thought of as wrath—is "a mere negation that will go up in smoke." As an inscription in mirror writing says in *Milton*, "Contraries are Positives. A Negation is not a Contrary."

Let us be as clear as possible: we have not shown that Blake stopped believing in contraries, but rather that such a belief became more and more difficult to sustain. The concept of Negation is a desperate measure intended to rescue the contraries by banishing from them whatever is irredeemably corrupt. But the act of banishment vitiates the whole meaning of contraries, either in Boehme's terms or in Hegel's. In the end we must probably conclude that Blake cannot organize the whole of his thought under the concept of contraries, and settles instead for different *kinds* of contraries, some of which are easily reconciled, others with great difficulty if at all. To put it differently, Blake's movement away from the optimistic "progression" of *The Marriage of Heaven and Hell* and toward the drastic exclusion of "negation" represents a recognition that much in our experience is radically unassimilable. Just as in his early annotations to Lavater he reserved the right to hate, so in his myth Blake remained true to the insight that prophetic wrath must treat some things as permanently unacceptable. No marriage of contraries can ultimately make all things one. Of course Blake often invokes Neoplatonic language to suggest that what he rejects never really existed at all; it is mere privation, like evil in Augustine and C. S. Lewis. But as the myth sufficiently expresses with dramatic if not logical force, the negation is all too real and its rejection is a real act of courage and imagination.

# Blake and Freud

*Diana Hume George*

*Songs of Experience* deals with the formation of culture and religion from the individual's perspective in the family unit. The oedipal configuration in *The First Book of Urizen* and *The Four Zoas* conflates the familial and the cultural. *The Marriage of Heaven and Hell*, published in 1793 (before the *Songs*) studies the same phenomena on the cosmic scale. The universal tensions Blake calls contraries are abstracted by society into morality.

> From these contraries spring what the religious call
> Good & Evil. Good is the passive that obeys Reason.
> Evil is the active springing from energy.
>   Good is Heaven. Evil is Hell.
>
>            (*The Marriage of Heaven and Hell*, plate 3)

Even Freud was never more succinct. Id impulses are designated as evil by society because their indulgence would retard the process of sublimation by which culture achieves its ends. "Energy" is Blake's id, and "the passive that obeys Reason" is the conservative trend in culture. It obeys Reason only at a great expenditure of energy, for unruly impulses must be constantly kept passive, latent, repressed. Good consists in obedience to the father in the family and to law and religion in society.

The *Marriage* says that all bibles and sacred codes teach falsehoods, among which is "that God will torment Man in Eternity for following his energies" (plate 4). This God is the same as Freud's God, who metes out punishment and reward for renunciation and sacrifice. "Those who restrain desire do so because theirs is weak enough to restrain; and the restrainer or reason usurps its place

---

From *Blake and Freud.* © 1980 by Cornell University. Cornell University Press, 1980.

and governs the unwilling. And being restrained it by degrees becomes passive till it is only the shadow of desire" (plate 5).

Freud calls the restraints of morality unjust for much the same reason. The demand is one that "one person can attain without effort, whereas it imposes on another the severest mental sacrifices." All men are originally the "unwilling" in Blake and Freud. "What makes itself felt in a human community as a desire for freedom . . . may (also) spring from the remains of their original personality, which is still untamed by civilization." The restraint works with the majority, yielding Blake's "shadow of desire" and Freud's neurotic personality, for whom "the return of the repressed" is experienced as illness.

When Blake's proverbs on desire are read against a backdrop of Freud's formulations on neurosis in society, their intent becomes clear. Undue suppression of sexuality is responsible for neurosis. "He who desires but acts not breeds pestilence" becomes intelligible as a cultural norm. The "pestilence" is neurosis in culture. Anyone who has ever tried to explain the sense of "Sooner murder an infant in its cradle than nurse unacted desire" might be grateful for Freud's support of what seems an inexplicably cruel metaphor. The human infant is murdered in its cradle when desire is unacted and therefore repressed, and the collective trend of nursing unacted desire in society kills the aim of human happiness, which ought to be the goal of civilization if it is to have any advantage whatever over an uncivilized state. "Damn. braces: Bless relaxes." "Expect poison from the standing water." "The road of excess leads to the palace of wisdom." "The tygers of wrath are wiser than the horses of instruction." "Prisons are built with stones of Law, Brothels with bricks of Religion."

That last proverb conflates and summarizes the fundamentals of Freud's findings on culture. Excessive strictness of law creates crime through suppression of instinct beyond a level the individual can tolerate. "No individual can keep these Laws, for they are death / To every energy of man" (*Jerusalem* 31:11–12). (If the capital *L* were removed from Laws and if the line break were absent, I wonder whether any student of Freud and Blake could guess which one had said it.) Religion creates prostitution by forbidding the indulgence of sexual appetite until marriage, and even after.

For Blake, the conflagration "will come to pass by an improvement of sensual enjoyment." Freud would agree that immediate gratification of impulse would bring about the destruction of the civilized world. But he would not advise it and would be horrified at the prospect. Blake thought civilization, as constituted, not worth the trouble necessary to maintain it. The revolution that destroys it will be a happy and holy one in which everything will "appear infinite" instead of "finite & corrupt." For Freud, the world appears finite and corrupt too, but its destruction would leave nothing of infinite value. It would leave nothing at all.

The creation of religion on the cultural level in *The Marriage of Heaven and Hell* is a derivative of the projective process. "The ancient Poets animated all sensible objects with Gods or Geniuses." They were "mental deities," but eventually a system was formed by abstraction of the deities from their objects. "Thus began Priesthood." The process is analogous to Freud's in *Totem and Taboo*. "Thus men forgot that All deities reside in the human breast." "Forgot" has much the same content as "repressed." The original mental deities were concentrated in the person of the father, and from the father of the family the God of culture was abstracted. "Primitive man," according to Freud, "transferred the structural relations of his own psyche to the outer world."

*The Marriage of Heaven and Hell* takes place on a mythic level in order to describe the contours of the holy as they took shape in the minds of men. Blake employed the concept of marriage to symbolize relationships between forces and principles, but he was equally attuned to the sociosexual relationship between men and women in his own society. He recognized marriage as the core relationship of the nuclear family, and therefore a cornerstone of civilization.

# Producers and Devourers

*Stewart Crehan*

Blake's brilliant intellectual satire and revolutionary tract, *The Marriage of Heaven and Hell* (*ca.* 1790–93) has attracted much critical commentary, but only a few interpretations have attempted to locate the work in its social context. One is Sabri-Tabrizi's *The "Heaven" and "Hell" of William Blake* (1973). Sabri-Tabrizi makes a number of important points, most of which seem to have been ignored by subsequent critics. The first is that "Heaven" and "Hell" "represent social classes and conditions." "Heaven" is the world of "the rich and propertied or higher clerical class," "Hell" is that of the poor and working class. This view is based on the discovery, through close reading, that Emmanuel Swedenborg's descriptions of Hell in his *Heaven and Hell* draw heavily, if unconsciously, on his knowledge of the coal mines he owned. Swedenborg's Heaven, on the other hand, is an idealised picture of the spacious world of the leisured upper classes. Since Blake's *Marriage* is in large part a satire on the writings and teachings of the founder of the New Church, Sabri-Tabrizi argues that Blake has seen through its theology as the worldly, predestinarian argument for an unjust social order. Whereas Swedenborg justified the condemnation of his "infernal spirits" (or workers) to a life in the "Hell" of his mines, Blake's sympathies are with those same spirits (whom he calls Devils, or producers), whose class-biased presentation he has exposed by his critical reading of the Swedish theologian's work. Swedenborg's New Church remains a defence of the older order; the "revival" of Blake's "Eternal Hell" is a positive response to the revolutionary upsurge of the oppressed.

Sabri-Tabrizi's thesis provides the starting-point for a critique of the usual run of idealist interpretations, according to which *The Marriage* is simply a celebration

From *Blake in Context.* © 1984 by Stewart Crehan. Gill and Macmillan Ltd., 1984. Humanities Press International, Inc., Atlantic Highlands, NJ.

of creative energy and the active imagination in opposition to reason and "materialistic" philosophy. In his commentary on the facsimile edition of *The Marriage* (Oxford University Press and the Trianon Press, 1975), for example, Geoffrey Keynes offers us the fully-rounded philosophy of an individual working in a socio-political vacuum: "To him [i.e., Blake] passive acceptance was evil, active opposition was good. This is the key to the meaning of the paradoxes and inversions of which the whole work consists." But *who* and *what* was Blake, and for whom was he writing? Can he be seen as some timeless, classless genius, ladling out universal prescriptions for everyone to follow? If, as Keynes says, Blake held to the principle that "active opposition is good," he must surely have welcomed the "active opposition" of the *ancien regime* to the Third Estate, the "active opposition" of the Tories to the movement for political reform, and the "active opposition" of Pitt to the French Republic in 1793 in the form of war preparations. Torn from its social and political context, Blake's *Marriage* is emptied of its living, revolutionary significance. The "active / passive" dualism makes little sense if we do not see that Blake was on the side of active, Republican-minded citizens, not "active" oppressors.

Reason and Energy, on the other hand, do have a universal significance. With these terms, Blake anticipated Freud's analysis of the ego and the id and their interrelations. Blake's polarities, like Freud's, draw attention to the *inner dynamics* of the psyche, overturning the mechanistic, undialectical model of the mind as comprising only the conscious and the pre-conscious, or latent memory. "Energy is the only life, and is from the Body; and Reason is the bound or outward circumference of Energy" conforms closely to Freud's topography, outlined in *The Ego and the Id* (1923), of the id as passion, bodily instinct and unconscious drives, and the ego as reason and common sense, or "that part of the id which has been modified by the direct influence of the external world." When Blake writes that those "who restrain desire, do so because theirs is weak enough to be restrained," and that "the restrainer or reason usurps its place & governs the unwilling," he is putting forward a theory of repression, which for Freud is the essential mechanism whereby the unconscious, including the pleasure principle, or "desire" (what Freud calls the libido) is governed and tamed by the reality principle. Blake asserts: "The tygers of wrath are wiser than the horses of instruction," and "the chains are the cunning of weak and tame minds which have power to resist energy." Freud confirms: "in its relation to the id [the ego] is like a man on horseback, who has to hold in check the superior strength of the horse; with this difference, that the rider tries to do so with his own strength while the ego uses borrowed forces." (Note that the Freudian id as instructed horse has been tamed; Blake's tigers have not.) Freud's categories are shorn of overt political meanings, though not of political implications; Blake's, however, are political through and through. Those who govern society and restrain the masses are the ones who, with their fiendish self-righteousness, have most effectively governed and restrained desire in themselves. This does not mean that they are therefore more rational, or that those who do not restrain desire in themselves are correspondingly less rational. If Reason is the outward circumference of Energy, then it may, by enclosing Energy in a narrower, more confined space, succeed in reducing it to "the shadow of desire," but in doing so it also diminishes itself. Such a law applies to political and social as much as it does to psychological repression. The typical ruling-class personality may be very good indeed at governing, taming and repressing, but in all other respects (such as in the sexual act, practical work that involves the body as well as the brain, artistic creation and all feats of the imagination) it may well be worse than useless.

"The Argument" of *The Marriage* opens cryptically:

> Rintrah roars & shakes his fires in the burdened air;
> Hungry clouds swag on the deep.

Sabri-Tabrizi argues at length that 'Rintrah' is Urizenic, a reactionary force; Keynes, on the other hand, says: " 'Rintrah' may be understood as 'Wrath,' the wrath of the poet-prophet, Blake himself." In the poem *Tiriel* (1789), Tiriel, the blind tyrant, calls upon "Thunder & fire & pestilence" to punish his rebellious sons:

> He ceast. The heavy clouds confusd rolld round the lofty towers
> Discharging their enormous voices. At the fathers curse
> The earth trembled fires belched from the yawning clefts
> And when the shaking ceast a fog possesst the accursed clime
> The cry was great in Tiriels palace.

In 1788 there had been an "aristocratic revolt" against Louis XVI, sparking off popular riots. In 1789 the political rift widened: it was not a dispute between the wealthy privileged orders and the King, but (as Rudé puts it) a *war* between the Third Estate and the two other orders. As the economic and political crisis deepened, the voice of the people began to be heard. Encouraged by outside popular pressure, the Third Estate (in effect, the revolutionary bourgeoisie) arrogated to itself the title of the National Assembly. This revolutionary act brought the masses further into play: on July 14 the Bastille itself fell.

Just as Tiriel's thunderous, fiery and pestilential curse on his "sons" makes the "earth" tremble and fires belch "from the yawning clefts" (echoed in the volcanic fires of the title-page to *The Marriage*), so the ideological and political conflicts between the minority ruling orders in France awakened deeper fires from "the yawning clefts" in society as a whole. Dismissing Sabri-Tabrizi's interpretation of the opening lines of "The Argument" as an allusion to the sulphurous, smoky air of Swedenborg's infernal coal mines, we can grasp the dialectical movement that the opening of Blake's *Marriage* enacts:

> Rintrah roars & shakes his fires in the burdened air:
> Hungry clouds swag on the deep.

> As a new heaven is begun, and it is now thirty-three years since its advent, the Eternal Hell revives.

(Thirty-three years is the time that has elapsed since the date of the New Jerusalem as announced by Swedenborg—that is, 1757, the year of Blake's birth—and it is also the age of Christ when he died.) Rintrah roars and hungry clouds "swag on the deep"; "a new heaven is begun" and "the Eternal Hell revives."

The dialectic here is that of the class struggle. The "above" and "below" of "burdened air" and "deep," "new heaven" and "Eternal Hell" indicate relationships of dominance, but the unity of opposites is not only political, the dominance of rulers overruled: it is based on the *appropriation* by the ruling few of what the governed many create. The line: "Hungry clouds swag on the deep" refers to an imminent thunderstorm at sea, in which "hungry" clouds, filled with too much moisture absorbed from "the deep," burden the air and are about to burst. (The dialect word "swag," meaning to hang swaying like a "bundle" or "fat belly" and from which is derived the noun "swag," meaning booty, and possibly "swagger," meaning to strut, has a radical force that the word "sway" would have lacked.) Later on, in "The Voice of the Devil" (plates 5–6), Blake gives us the "history" of the usurpation of power by "Reason" from two ideological viewpoints, that of the rulers and that of the ruled: "It indeed appear'd to Reason as if Desire was cast out, but the Devil's account is, that the Messiah fell, & formed a heaven of what he stole from the Abyss." Here "the Governor, or Reason" (Milton's "Messiah") is the "fallen" usurper; the "Heaven" of the rationalists (whom Blake the libertarian sees as ideologues for an existing social order) was formed out of the *stolen* products that those deep in the social "Abyss" created. (It is worth remembering at this point that Blake's "diabolical" wit and mode of argument defy logical or systematic analysis. There is much in *The Marriage* that is comic, while Blake's satiric "Devil" persona delights in a disruptive presentation, throwing off brilliantly memorable verbal sparks with that subversive intellectual audacity that is typical of a certain kind of anarchic individualism, or what Blake would have called "Poetic Genius," possessed only by those who follow their "Energies.")

Plates 16–17 are a highly suggestive amalgam of related ideas presented in extremely condensed form. Taken with the passages so far discussed, they further illuminate the Blakean dialectic:

The Giants who formed this world into its sensual existence and now seem to live in it in chains, are in truth the causes of its life & the sources of all activity; but the chains are the cunning of weak and tame minds which have power to resist energy, according to the proverb, the weak in courage is strong in cunning.

Thus one portion of being is the Prolific, the other the Devouring: to the devourer it seems as if the producer was in his chains; but it is not so, he only takes portions of existence and fancies that the whole.

But the Prolific would cease to be Prolific unless the Devourer, as a sea, received the excess of his delights. . .

These two classes of men are always upon earth, & they should be enemies: whoever tries to reconcile them seeks to destroy existence.

Religion is an endeavour to reconcile the two.

The deeper implications of this passage will be examined later. The argument is as follows: the "Giants who formed this world into its sensual existence" and are "the sources of all activity" seem to live in it in chains. These chains "are the cunning of weak and tame minds" who have power to resist the energy of prolific creators. But the chains, we are told, are in fact illusory. It is only through the myopic, false consciousness of the devourer that the producer seems to be in his chains. Far from chaining him, this dependence on the devourer releases the producer's prolific energies. The unequal relationship turns out to be absolutely necessary, since for the producer to produce to excess, he must have devourers who can receive "the excess of his delights." (We shall return to this paradox later.) Finally, we are told that producers and devourers are "two classes of men" irreconcilably opposed, and that it is the utopian mission of "religion" to achieve a reconciliation between them (that is, by blurring or smoothing the class contradictions).

The question arises: Who are Blake's "Giants" and prolific producers? Are they, as Sabri-Tabrizi argues, the poor and the working class? Before attempting an immediate answer, let us set against Blake's radical historiography a more consistent exposition by a writer with whom he is now often (and often too loosely) compared—Gerrard Winstanley, the writer who has a prime claim to the title of the first English socialist. Winstanley's *The True Levellers' Standard Advanced* (1649) opens:

In the beginning of time, the great creator Reason made the earth to be a common treasury, to preserve beasts, birds, fishes and man, the Lord that was to govern this creation. . . .

But since human flesh (that king of beasts) began to delight himself in the objects of the creation, more than in the spirit of reason and righteousness . . . he fell into blindness of mind and weakness of heart, and runs abroad for a teacher and ruler. And so selfish imagination . . . did set up one man to teach and rule over another. . . . And hereupon the earth . . . was hedged into enclosures by the teachers and rulers, and the others were made servants and slaves: and the earth, that is within this creation made a common storehouse for all, is bought and sold and kept in the hands of a few, whereby the great creator is mightily dishonoured, as if he were a respecter of persons, delighting in the comfortable livelihood of some, and rejoicing in the miserable poverty and straits of others. From the beginning it was not so.

Winstanley presents an unambiguous and lucid account of how mankind came to be divided into classes: "teachers and rulers" on the one hand, and "servants and slaves" on the other, arose on the basis of private property in the means of production, which for Winstanley is always the land and the means for tilling it. A spokesman for the dispossessed landless laborers of the seventeenth century, Winstanley anticipates the method of modern historical materialism. His "contraries" compare interestingly with Blake's: it is not Reason that usurps Desire, but "selfish imagination" that usurps "the great creator Reason," while instead of "the Devouring" and "the Prolific" we have "teachers and rulers," "servants and slaves"—explicit class categories.

The originality of Blake's terms shows that he is trying to describe a new historical phenomenon—in particular, the Radical, plebeian intellectual and self-educated artist or craftsman who is now emerging as a potent force for change. (The revival of "the Eternal Hell" of Radicalism, dead since 1784, occurred in 1790 when Horne Tooke got 1,779 votes at the Westminster election. Westminster, where Blake lived, "was one of the few 'open' constituencies in the south of England, with a householder franchise which admitted many master-artisans and some journeymen to the vote.") In other words, the "producer" whom The Marriage chiefly celebrates is not the dispossessed labourer, peasant or "chained" servant, but the prolifically creative, Radical artist-craftsman or artisan who, as an "active citizen" (at least in Westminster), struggles to free himself, his fellow-producers, and hence society as a whole, from the economic, political, moral and aesthetic constraints of the old aristocratic, monarchical system.

The poetic resonance of Blake's categories ("Giants," "Prolific," "Devouring")—that is, their lack of historical concreteness and social specificity (which are the hallmark of other radical writers from Winstanley through Rousseau to Paine)—is indicative of an individualistic and subjective desire for liberation. In the passage we have quoted, the deep structure of Blake's argument, with its idea of a usurpation giving rise to dialectical oppositions, is the same as

Winstanley's. Like many "liberation" texts, it offers an explanation of the present order in terms of a historical usurpation leading to a system that is the "contrary" or polar inversion of an original human condition. Man's original creative energies have been usurped by rational scepticism, the dominance of "Hell" by that of "Heaven," the paramountcy of "Giants" by the rule of "weak and tame minds." The rhetorical method, vocabulary and style of Blake's illuminated text, however, with its sudden breaks and transitions, its mixing of modes (such as poetry, philosophy and satire), and its proliferation of linearly related, "contrary" categories (Reason/Energy → Soul/Body → Restraint/Desire → Angel/Devil → Devourer/Producer, etc.) enact an urgent, *subjective* need to break with the old forms, not only through a radical philosophy or radical politics, but through a radical aesthetic. The visual impact and originality of *The Marriage,* with its plentitude of pictorial and typographical meanings, the power of its language (where new associations, based on semantic transformations, are deliberately exploited), are as important to Blake as any "objective," prosaic meaning. This is not simply a question of aesthetics, for politics and aesthetics are always intertwined. The aesthetics and style of *The Marriage* cannot, then, be excluded in the attempt to define its class viewpoint and the social conditions of its appearance: its readers must produce its meanings.

Our task has been made easier in one way by the self-consciousness of the text. The first "Memorable Fancy," relating in travelogue style how the narrator has collected some "Proverbs of Hell," is an ironic parody of Swedenborg's "Memorable Relations." This has led readers and critics into not taking the narrator seriously, that is, literally—the "Blakean" Hell being thought of only metaphorically and not as a real place. In fact, Blake's Hell does have, and indeed *must* have, a real social location. (This is to read *The Marriage,* as Blake's Devil reads the Bible, in its "infernal or diabolical sense." There are too many "Angelic" readers of Blake.) The text reads as follows:

> As I was walking among the fires of hell, delighted with the enjoyments of Genius, which to Angels look like Torment and insanity, I collected some of their Proverbs; thinking that as the sayings used in a nation mark its character, so the Proverbs of Hell show the nature of Infernal wisdom better than any description of buildings or garments.

The narrator (a mock-genteel persona) has discovered in this "Infernal wisdom" a rich subculture (or what might be termed a "counter-culture" or "radical culture"). He is conveying to us some of the oral literature ("sayings") of a nation within a nation. In this sense, we are being asked to attribute the "Proverbs of Hell" not to the genius of a single individual, but to the "Infernal wisdom" of the creative majority. (It is interesting to note, incidentally, that Blake did not sign *The Marriage* with his usual "The Author & Printer W Blake.") The proverbs are meant to be taken as the varied living utterances of "Devils" whose physical (and in this must be included sexual) energies (Energy being "the only life" and "from the Body") are the inexhaustible wellsprings of infernal culture, a culture that is both Jacobin and antinomian. As Lindsay points out, "English Jacobins called the Devil the first Jacobin."

Infernal culture, expressing the energy of active producers, is, however, essentially individualistic, despite the solidarity the real, historical "Devils" might have displayed as a class, their sense of community, or the interdependent nature of the productive process. Blake lived, in fact, in an extremely competitive environment. On May 28, 1804 he told Hayley: "In London every calumny and falsehood utter'd against another of the same trade is thought fair play. Engravers, Painters, Statuaries, Printers, Poets, we are not in a field of battle, but a City of Assassinations." The proverb: "The most sublime act is to set another before you" suggests that for a Devil, taking a back seat requires some effort (though a Devil in the fifth "Memorable Fancy" says that the worship of God is "Honouring his gifts in other men, each according to his genius, and loving the greatest men best"). "No bird soars too high, if he soars with his own wings" assumes that each man's gifts are *his own*, not God's or society's; "The apple tree never asks the beech how he shall grow; nor the lion, the horse, how he shall take his prey" combines both the idea of sovereign intellect's independence from "the horses of instruction" and the principle that each man must follow his individual genius. Both A. L. Morton and Christopher Hill have emphasised Blake's connection with the "left-wing" radicals of the seventeenth century. However, in *The Marriage* he is arguably closer to the anarchic individualism of the Ranters (whose support derived largely from freed migratory craftsmen, men who were "unattached and prepared to break with tradition," according to Morton) than he is to the Diggers' peasant collectivism, whose spirit still lives in the writings of Gerrard Winstanley, a man of profound socialist instincts.

The third "Memorable Fancy" informs us that the culture of "Hell" is not only oral, but includes technical means for spreading its "Infernal wisdom" (something Pitt and the Tories, with their spies and censors, were eager to put an end to). The visit to a "Printing house in hell" takes us through the process of the transmission of knowledge "from generation to generation." The printing house is, on one level, Blake's own workshop. But to argue (with one critic, W. J. T. Mitchell) that it is Blake's own "cavernous skull that is being cleared of rubbish . . . [and] made infinite by imaginative labor"; that the "books which result from this labor come from a printing house in a cave, but they also come out of a *head*," while passing over the reference to the work of the type-founder (in the *melting* of "*metals* into living fluids" which are then *cast* "into the expanse"), obscures the premise that creative labor, or Energy, "is from the Body," and that such work cannot occur merely in the "cave" of one's own skull, but is practical and social.

Behind Blake's account of how books are made, with its allegorical personifications (reminiscent of alchemical texts), lies an urban, radical culture, a world of political theorists, journalists and pamphleteers, also engaged in "clearing away the rubbish" of dead ideas; a milieu of "progressive" illustrators, decorative artists, poets, painters, engravers, type-founders, compositors, copper-plate printers, book-binders, book-sellers, antiquarians and librarians. Blake's own "infernal method" of printing was a stereotype process he himself (soaring with "his own wings") developed, though others had hit on the idea independently. (In this period, technical innovation and experiment were invariably carried out by practical men: apart from Watt's modifications to the steam engine, which were the result of formal scientific experiment, and industrial processes such as bleaching and dyeing, which were the result of advances in chemistry, none of the major inventions of the industrial revolution were the results of advances in theoretical science.) Blake deserves the appellation of Renaissance Artist, however, since he combined in his work the trades of copper-plate printer, book-binder, book-seller, print-seller, painter, engraver and philosopher, together with the unclassifiable pursuits of prophet and poet, though perhaps "Poetic Genius," being the whole man, embraces all these activities.

Blake's "Prolific" or "Devils," then, are not producers of the means of subsistence, though most are practical men who use their hands; they are, in the main, producers of *art* and of *ideas*, men of "Poetic Genius" who have allied themselves with the energy and the cause of the working masses. They are, in sum, the new petty-bourgeois and lower-class democratic intelligentsia. The printer and the book-seller (the latter often combining the functions of proprietor and publisher), were key figures in this radical milieu. Prolific book-sellers and publishers in Paternoster Road and St Paul's Church-yard—men such as Joseph Johnson, who published Wordsworth and Mary Wollstonecraft as well as Paine's *Rights of Man*—were of central importance to the whole cause of English Radicalism. "It is to such men," wrote the author of *The Young Tradesman* in 1824, "[that] our men of genius take their productions for sale: and the success of works of genius very frequently depends upon their spirit, probity, and patronage . . . it is by the diffusion of knowledge by books that all species of tyranny and oppression can be most effectively resisted" (a view, of course, that ignores the role of newspapers, and also presumes a literate population). Blake's allegorical description of "the method in which knowledge is transmitted from generation to generation" could be seen as supporting that view; however, after

1790 (when Johnson had printed, but did not publish, Blake's *French Revolution*)
Blake was always his own printer and book-seller—not out of some Crusoe-
like, do-it-yourself crankiness, but for important artistic and ideological reasons.

The role of the printer (whether copper-plate or using type) in artisan London (in which "the chief trades," according to Sir John Clapham, were, apart
from the building trades, the "shoemaker, tailor, cabinet-maker, printer, clock-
maker, jeweller, [and] baker") was significant in various ways. W. H. Reid,
truly one of Blake's Tory "Angels," tells us that Swedenborgianism as an "infidel" movement originated "in a printer's job" in the parish of Clerkenwell.
Its next appearance was "in an alley in Little Eastcheap, partly in the modern
and fashionable form of a debating society: but, instead of preachers collecting
the people, these people were so hard run to collect preachers, that for a considerable time the office was generally confined to the printer alluded to, and
one of his relatives." (*The Marriage of Heaven and Hell* was conventionally printed;
Blake printed and colored his copies of *The Marriage of Heaven and Hell* in a singular-
ly unconventional "printer's job.")

We know that Blake attended an early London meeting of the Swedenborgian New Church in 1789, and that within a year he was satirising Swedenborg in *The Marriage of Heaven and Hell.* Two other men, one a carpenter called
John Wright, the other a copper-plate printer called William Bryan, also recorded
their disillusionment with the New Church. Wright tells us of his visit to the
"Jerusalem Church" in 1788, in Great Eastcheap:

> The Sunday following, so called, I went to the place, where I saw
> nothing but old *forms* of worship established by *man's will*, and not
> according to the will of GOD, although called by that blessed name
> of *New Jerusalem*, in which these old forms have neither part nor
> lot. I saw no one there, except the preacher, whom I knew; he had
> been a preacher among *John Wesley's* people.

This compares closely with Blake's rejection of Swedenborg's "old forms" in
*The Marriage:* "And lo! Swedenborg is the Angel sitting at the tomb: his writings are the linen clothes folded up." In October 1788 Wright and Bryan felt
the call for a radical change in their lives. As Wright puts it: "a burning wind
is spreading over the earth, and wouldest thou leave to its ravages those whom
thou canst save?" In 1789 the Holy Spirit told both men to visit "a Society
at *Avignon* who were favoured with divine communications." Bryan records
the event:

> The 23rd of the month called January, 1789, in the morning, hav-
> ing made all things ready for my work, which was then copper-plate

printing, I found a stop in my mind to go on with it. Waiting a
little, I took some paper to wet for another plate, but found the same
stop: then I perceived that it was of the Lord. Retiring into my little room, I sat down, endeavouring to get my mind into perfect
stillness, when a voice spoke in me, commanding me to prepare for
my journey, that night.

The humble copper-plate printer, who has to make prints from plates others
have engraved, hears the voice of the Lord telling him to leave his work and
embark on a journey. William Blake, an engraver who felt the same need for
radical change, continued the ideological struggle (which, particularly in England,
so often took a sectarian form) through his art, "printing," as he says in *The
Marriage,* "in the infernal method, by corrosives, which in Hell are salutary and
medicinal"—that is, exposing reactionary dogma with corrosive, burning acid
in his new etching process. Instead of God's voice, it is "The Voice of the Devil"
that *he* hears. Blake's antinomian and immanentist rejection of a Lord who is
above or without (he has learned from Swedenborg that the divine and the human
are one, and hence that "All deities reside in the human breast") was the first
step in overcoming that mental self-division of those who saw their lives, minds
and actions governed by "the Lord," "Angels," "the Holy Spirit" and so forth.

Blake's increasing self-sufficiency as an artist-craftsman is mirrored in his
philosophical independence and a conviction that the rule of kings and priests
is ending, a conviction that has, of course, to be seen as part of the wider revolutionary movement. As Reid puts it, the 1790s were a new era in England "because
it delineates the first period in which the doctrines of Infidelity have been exten-
sively circulated among the lower orders." Although Reid includes Swedenborg
among the "Infidels," Blake puts him with the religious conformists: "He conversed with Angels who are all religious, & conversed not with Devils who all
hate religion, for he was incapable thro' his conceited notions." Blake corroborates
Reid in one respect, however, for his Devils, like Reid's "infidel" lower orders,
"all hate religion."

William Sharp, a friend of Blake and a follower of the millenarian Richard
Brothers and later of Joanna Southcott, was an engraver whose struggle for independence (not wholly achieved in terms of an original art, however) closely
parallels that of Blake, and tells us something about the conflict between "producers" and "devourers" within the print trade itself. According to W. S. Baker,
Sharp "became dissatisfied with the remuneration he received from the print
dealers." (Normally the engraver merely copied an artist's design, which was
then printed on a press belonging to the copper-plate printer, after which the
prints were sold to the print-dealer or print-shop owner.) Just as Blake was able
to buy a printing press on the death of his father in 1784, so Sharp,

becoming possessed of some property, by the decease of a brother,
began to publish his own works. Soon afterwards, about the year
1787, that date appearing on his print of "Zenobia," he moved to
a larger house in Charles St., near the Middlesex hospital.

Sharp, like Blake, had at least broken free of the chains of the print-dealers, who
exerted a financial and aesthetic hold over artists and engravers. Catering for
the tastes and fashions of middle-class print-buyers (part of the great consuming—
that is, "devouring"—public), the dealers, like the orthodox patrons and con-
noisseurs, took aesthetic "portions of existence" and fancied those the whole.
Sharp, like Blake, showed—once a degree of independence as a creative "producer" had been achieved—that the interests of the producers were quite different from those of the devourers. Instead of picturesque scenes, copies of paintings by Reynolds, West and the like, he could engrave portraits of the people's
heroes, such as Richard Brothers, Tom Paine and Horne Tooke, and publish
prints from his own drawings. Such a career brought with it, of course, the
threat of punishment in a very real, earthly "dungeon." Like Blake later, Sharp
was arrested, being brought before members of the privy council in 1794–95
on suspicion of having "revolutionary principles."

Unless the artist-craftsman could free himself from the dictates of Tory patrons
and the tastes of the buyers (however lucrative that subservience might prove),
there could be no cleansed perception, no overflowing fountain of "infernal"
culture. Yet at this point the Romantic paradox appears: to whom could the
revolutionary artist convey his "infinite" perceptions if not to a "devouring" public?
With astonishing far-sightedness, anticipating Marx, Blake is able to perceive
the dilemma in terms of an *irreconcilable* enmity between "two classes of men."
Historically, this enmity can be explained by the fact that the producer became
divorced from an abstract, impersonal and unknown public by the mechanism
of the market. The Blakean free artist, the man who had freed himself from
the oppressor's law and from spiritual repression, and who exercised his Poetic
Genius without restraint, had become locked in a "marriage" of enmity with
those passive "devourers" on whom, as an artist, he had to depend for a living.
The contradiction was insoluble: "These two classes of men are always upon
earth." Whereas Keats, Shelley and Wordsworth showed a certain elitist disdain as poets for "the foolish crowd" and the "unthinking" Public, Blake's class
position enabled him to see this relationship dialectically. (Yet the Romantic
disdain for his readers is there when his "Devil" says: "I have also The Bible
of Hell, which the world shall have whether they will or no.")

Blake articulates in *The Marriage* and *A Song of Liberty* the same kind of
revolutionary spirit that inspired the actions of the citizens of Paris in 1789. Writing

at around the same time as Blake, Paine recalled how the masses armed themselves prior to the assault on the Bastille:

> The night was spent in providing themselves with every sort of weapon they could make or procure: Guns, swords, blacksmiths' hammers, carpenters' axes, iron crows, pikes, halberts, pitchforks, spits, clubs, &c. &c. The incredible numbers in which they assembled the next morning, and the still more incredible resolution they exhibited, embarrassed and astonished their enemies. Little did the new ministry expect such a salute. Accustomed to slavery themselves, they had no idea that Liberty was capable of such inspiration, or that a body of unarmed citizens would dare to face the military force of thirty thousand men.

Just as the creatively inspired, revolutionary artisans of Paris had used blacksmiths' hammers, carpenters' axes and iron crows as weapons, so Blake turned his own art into a weapon. It came to possess the same qualities of imaginative daring, skill, energy, resolution, and capacity for seizing the moment that were shown by the revolutionaries in France. All it lacked (and this was Blake's predicament as an artist) was the mass readership that Paine was able to reach. Yet, imaginatively inspired as the citizens of Paris were inspired, Blake was even able to see his own alienation from the art-buying and poetry-reading public as a dialectical contradiction, part of a wider class struggle.

Blake's *Marriage* reflects a new awareness that social existence is riven by "yawning clefts," and hence into two opposed ways of seeing, two ideological camps. To the revolutionary artist, for whom sharply distinct outlines are an aesthetic imperative, whoever tries to reconcile these viewpoints "seeks to destroy existence." It is with this *ideological* split that Blake's *Marriage* is chiefly concerned. Just as a "fool sees not the same tree that a wise man sees," so devouring Angels and prolific Devils perceive the world in wholly different ways. Blake's Angel sees the French Revolution as a terrifying monster rising from the depths of society, a Leviathan whose "mouth & red gills" hang "just above the raging foam, tinging the black deep with beams of blood." (The "Hungry clouds" that "swag on the deep" in the opening free-verse "Argument" have now burst: "the deep", from which those devouring clouds absorbed their moisture, and from which the upper-class Anglican clergy stole in order to form their "Heaven," has now turned into a "raging foam.") The Angel hears and sees in the Revolution "a terrible noise" and a huge monster; but Blake finds himself "sitting on a pleasant bank beside a river by moonlight, hearing a harper, who sung to the harp." What to conservative Angels is a cacophony of noise (the noise of the "rabble") is to him pleasant music.

Blake's preoccupation with ideology and modes of perception, reflecting his class position, also informs his account of the origin of priesthood:

> The ancient Poets animated all sensible objects with Gods or Geniuses, calling them by the names and adorning them with the properties of woods, rivers, mountains, lakes, cities, nations, and whatever their enlarged & numerous senses could perceive. . . .
>
> Till a system was formed, which some took advantage of, & enslav'd the vulgar by attempting to realise or abstract the mental deities from their objects: thus began Priesthood:
>
> Choosing forms of worship from poetic tales.
>
> And at length they pronounc'd that the Gods had order'd such things.
>
> Thus men forgot that All deities reside in the human breast.

The original-state-*versus*-usurpation idea is in line with previous "radical" explanations of the origin of priesthood. But for writers such as Winstanley, Diderot and Rousseau, those priests who "enslav'd the vulgar" by using religion to defend an unjust social order were—in the words of the English radicals of the seventeenth century—preeminently "*tithing* priests," whose reliance on rent, tithes, and feudal dues made them obvious targets for class hatred. Blake's explanation: "thus began Priesthood," is, of course, an idealist one: ideology (the abstraction of "mental deities from their objects") precedes class formation ("Priesthood"). Nevertheless, Blake anticipates Marx by showing how a "fantastical realm" of institutionalised ideas is directly linked to the rise of an unproductive class.

The antinomy of producer and devourer in *The Marriage* contains an important ambiguity, which has so far only been touched upon. That is, it can be read either as producer/consumer or as producer/*exploiter*. Both meanings are present. The ambiguity exists for us, where it did not exist for Blake, because the historical distinction between wage worker and capitalist—particularly in London, that vast hive of small workshops—had not yet sufficiently hardened. In Blake's later work, the ambiguity is partly resolved.

The ideological moment of *The Marriage* can also be felt in Blake's doctrine of "contraries" and in his notion of "excess." Blake's dialectic, which owes more to the spiritual "contraries" of Jacob Boehme than it does to the alchemical (and hence, more "materialist") contraries of Paracelsus, is both radical and conservative. Underlying the whole satiric purpose of *The Marriage* is the semantic transformation of terms such as "good" and "evil," "Heaven" and "Hell." But does the transformation (the "Evil" of Energy becoming "Eternal Delight") leave us with a new set of eternally fixed oppositions, such that idealist readings of *The Marriage* appear as the most "natural" ones to take? If the "contraries" of

Heaven and Hell, Reason and Energy, are eternally "married," locked together for all time, then does this not also apply to those "social classes and conditions" which, as Sabri-Tabrizi has argued, they represent? This surely turns Blake into a Swedenborgian. *A Song of Liberty* clearly calls for the *ending* of tyranny, Empire, and the rule of "the lion & the wolf." Yet the ambiguity (Is *class* society, though perceived from the "abyss" up and not from the top down, nevertheless reaffirmed, when the class struggle is seen as eternal?) remains. Given its historical and political context, *The Marriage* could not have gone as far in its critique as Winstanley did almost 150 years before.

Finally, the notion of "excess," that well-known agent of social disorder, needs to be set in its ideological context. At one level, "excess" is going "beyond" or transcending oneself; a kind of Dionysiac ecstacy or surplus energy that cannot be contained or rationalised, a feeling of being at one with prolific creation. This has nothing in common with hedonism or libertinism, the moralist's idea of excess as intemperance or over-indulgence. The proverb: "The road of excess leads to the palace of wisdom" contains at one level the Dionysian belief that another, higher order of "wisdom," of spiritual knowledge and perception, can be attained through libidinal "excess" or ecstatic self-abandon. Excess is, of course, fundamental to the spirit of Romanticism. Yet instead of viewing it as part of the universal human need for transcendental experiences (which can only be realised outside the work process), the principle of excess, looked at from a more "earthly" angle, might be seen to have an *immanent,* work-oriented side to it.

In *The Marriage*, Blake says: "the Prolific would cease to be the Prolific unless the Devourer, as a sea, received the excess of his delights" (where "as a sea" has an ironic twist). A. S. Vasquez points out that under the new, "freed" conditions of artistic production, the Romantic artist "had to produce a number of works that exceeded, in quantity and economic value, what he needed in order to survive." Blake's notion of creative excess, either as a productive surplus ("the excess of his delights"), or as a prolific, bountiful giving, in the sense in which God and nature are prolific and bountiful (hence: "The lust of the goat is the bounty of God") can be connected with an important shift in eighteenth-century economic thought, as the dominance of mercantile gave way to industrial capital.

Mercantilist theories had derived the source of profit (or excess wealth) from the circulation sphere, that is, exchange of commodities (buying cheap and selling dear). Profit (always a definite, measurable quantity of money) owed its existence to the laws of the market and to the business skills of the merchant. The Physiocrats, on the other hand, saw that mercantile profit could not involve the creation of *new* wealth, since it was simply a redistribution of wealth already created, and therefore, as Blake might have put it, "unable to do other than repeat the same dull round over again." The source of society's wealth, and hence of the social surplus, thus lies in the sphere, not of *exchange*, but of *production*. It is through the agricultural producers, those who tap the inexhaustible bounties of nature, that a marketable surplus is created, and *this* surplus is not merely monetary profit; it is the living and essential foundation upon which the whole of civilised life—in other words, the aristrocracy, the clergy, commerce, the professions, and the whole of urban life—depends.

In Physiocratic theory (so-called because of the importance it attached to nature, *phusis* in Greek), the farmer is only able to create a surplus (i.e., what is surplus to his needs) through the bounty of nature. It is not labour but nature itself that is prolific. Man only intervenes; he taps the vital source. He becomes prolific by virtue of his closeness to nature. The natural process of germination, growth, flowering and bearing fruit, made possible by the combined action of nutrients in the soil, heat from the sun and moisture from the rain, is the basis of life and hence of all wealth; it is the overflowing fountain in the human economy. The Rousseauesque "natural man," simple, free and spontaneous; the Romantic cult of nature; the quasi-mystical notion of prolific nature working through man (as opposed to man working on nature); even Wordworth's characterization of poetry as "the spontaneous overflow of powerful feelings" (where the "feelings" are "nature's")—all these can be connected with the Physiocrats' discovery that prolific nature and the farmer are the source of the social surplus.

Physiocratic theory emerged at a time when the bourgeoisie, not yet a class acting for itself, was incapable of carrying through a major political change, yet the theory contained a systematic and far-reaching critique of existing society, which could now be seen to be divided into productive and unproductive classes. Those who were productive produced in excess of their requirements. The unproductive classes merely consumed, distributed or changed the form of the surplus produced by the productive classes. For the representatives of the bourgeoisie and petty-bourgeoisie, however, such a theory was in need of drastic modification, since it made all the non-agricultural classes dependent and even parasitic upon the bounties of nature, made serviceable by the investment and labor of the farmer. Adam Smith extended the Physiocrats' categories to every sphere in which *productive capital* was employed, these spheres being agriculture, trade and manufacture. (Here it is *capital*, not simply labour itself, that is productive.) The concept of productive labour was held to mean any labour that was *put to work by capital* (since capital involves an increased return on investment).

The position of the Physiocrats and followers of Rousseau might be summed up in the maxim: "Where nature is not, man is barren." Blake's "proverb of Hell" is a reversal of this: "Where *man* is not, *nature* is barren." In a craft and artisan environment, the emphasis shifts from the fertility of nature to human productivity, from prolific nature to prolific work. The craftsman does not rely on the bounties of nature in order to be prolific or productive, but on his own *human* energies. (The Physiocrats would retort: Then how does he eat? To which Adam Smith would reply that any commodity, even a book, has an economic value.)

In Blake's mythological epics, the most "progressive" figures are Los, a blacksmith-prophet, and his female "Emanation," Enitharmon, who weaves at her loom. In *Milton* it is Los who must first "forge the instruments / Of Harvest" (the plough and harrow) for Palamabron the ploughman—a nice reversal of the Physiocratic order. It is not the ploughman—who is also Blake the engraver, ploughing "furrows" on a copper plate with his graving tool—who is the guiding creative force in Blake's scheme of things, but Los, struggling to create "Definite Form" with "Hammer & Tongs" as he labours "at his resolute Anvil." Los, not Palamabron, is the archetype of the creative producer. (There is an interesting parallel here with the Nigerian dramatist, novelist and poet Wole Soyinka. Ogun, the Yoruba god of iron and of all those who work with iron, is the poet's guiding inspiration and source of creative energy. See, for example, the long poem *Idanre*, where Ogun is celebrated as divine creator and destroyer.)

In Blake's poetic myth Adam Smith is rebutted along with the Physiocrats, since labour that is unwilling or is carried out in the service of some master can never be creative, just as any artistic work that is the slave of "fashionable Fools" or a particular, ready-made market will be on the side of that "Class of Men whose whole delight is in Destroying." Nor is art quantifiable. It is (to use Marx's terms) a use-value, not an exchange value. Thus what Blake means by being "prolific" is not producing a merely *quantitative* excess, but striving for a better world through genuine works of art, combinations of words, sounds and images that awaken a new, enlarged perception of reality, and whose creation springs from a deep physical and emotional need, which is also a *social* need.

Blake's class affinities and his own work process—preparing the copper plate, seeing his reflection as a "mighty Devil" in its mirror-like surface, applying the "corrosive fires" of acid or ploughing its surface with his burin, making the imprint by turning the wheel of his press, mixing his colours—all this called up a poetic reverie that, while it actively participated in and urged on the work, also evoked other kinds of work, and at the same time inspired certain archetypal images and symbols. As Gaston Bachelard has shown, this kind of reverie or day-dreaming has a phenomenological aspect, in that, while he is freely associating, the "dreamer" is physically working with actual material substances. By getting to know their inner life, their secret virtues and mysterious habits (such as the extent of metallic resistance to the pressure of the cutting edge, the quantity of water and pigment needed to get the right viscosity, etc.) the "mystical" artist-craftsman sees them obeying his will, which to him is spiritual and not governed by mechanical laws. His spiritual will enters these substances, and they in turn enter him. Thus a dialectic unfolds. His artistic will is akin to that of a creator-god, yet a god who is *in* his creation: the artist engages, at an imaginative level, in the work of cosmic creation and the cosmic process itself, in which he is both maker and made. In his cosmic mythology, he comes to see that the creation—which includes himself—is only kept going by his own kind of imaginative labour. Without it, the sun would not rise, or give off spear-like rays like those from a blacksmith's hammer when it sets. Thus the Paracelsan, hermetic view that man's reason alone cannot penetrate nature's mysteries. Their unveiling must bring into play deeper levels of the psyche. In the alchemical work of imaginative creation, "matter" is infused with "spirit," including that of the divine artist himself. His energetic will fashions, animates and gives inner meaning to his creation, which appears infinite to all those who give themselves, as Los gives himself, through inspired, imaginative labour. This process—especially when fire and considerable energy are required—is one of conflict and struggle, as Bachelard says:

> If passively, as an idle visitor, you find yourself in the stifling atmosphere surrounding a china kiln, then the *anguish of heat* [cf. Blake's "furnaces of affliction"] takes hold of you. You retreat. You do not want to look any longer. You are afraid of the sparks. You think it is hell.
>
> Nevertheless, move closer. Take on in your imagination the work of the artisan. Imagine yourself putting the wood into the oven: cram the oven with shovels-full of coal, challenge the oven to a duel of energy. In short, be ardent and the ardor of the hearth will shoot its arrows in vain against your chest; you will be invigorated by the struggle. The fire can only return your blows. The psychology of *opposition* invigorates the worker. . . .
>
> Take away dreams and you stultify the worker. Leave out the oneiric force of work and you diminish, you annihilate the artisan. Each labor has its oneirism, each material worked on contributes its inner reveries. . . . The oneirism of work is the very condition of the worker's mental integrity.

Under conditions of capitalist production, with its increasing division of labour, where labour is *abstract* labour, "creative labour" becomes less and less possible. (One of the characteristically "Urizenic" features of bourgeois economic science is the way it turns human needs into dehumanising constraints, the whole man's creative excess into calculable "portions" called profit margins.) On the other hand, the "craft" viewpoint tends to belittle the working class (not fully born as an organised movement in Blake's time) as an agent of its own liberation; dehumanised by the new work discipline, with its reduction of factory worker into "hands," the exploited labourers have to rely on the visions of the inspired few. Yet Blake's viewpoint as a direct producer allowed him to see with "prophetic" insight that labour (one of the most frequently used words in his longer poems), though enslaving under conditions of enforced drudgery, is at the same time the key to man's liberation—*labour,* not merely "imagination," and certainly not *nature.*

# Roads of Excess

*Robert F. Gleckner*

Frye's fine essay entitled "The Road of Excess" was succeeded a year later by Martin Price's book *To the Palace of Wisdom.* Although the latter does not refer to the former, both titles come from one of Blake's famous Proverbs of Hell in *The Marriage of Heaven and Hell:* "The road of excess leads to the palace of wisdom." Frye's allusion, in his half of the proverb, is to the extremity of "Blake's statements about art," which demands "some kind of mental adjustment to take them in." Price, on the other hand, says that the proverb reminds us "that all literature thrives on risk and overstatement, thrusts beyond the measured and judicious, and strains against order, if only to make us know what measure and order mean." With both of these applications in mind I too take up Blake's proverb, in an attempt to provide a critical entrée into an odd *ménage à deux* indeed—Blake and Spenser in the "house" of *The Marriage of Heaven and Hell.*

Although all sensible Blakeans acknowledge that *The Marriage* is some sort of satire, the butt of which (Swedenborg) is merely a target of convenience or avenue to much larger concerns, I for one am dissatisfied with all interpretations of the work—which are, perhaps for reasons that I shall adduce here, not particularly numerous, given its apparent centrality and seminal nature in the canon—not because they *mis*read exactly but because no guiding principle of interpretation has yet been advanced that will account for the apparent shifts in the authoritativeness of the several speakers. More simply, when is Blake speaking "in his own voice," and how do we know? In posing to himself the same question ("Where does Blake speak straight?"), Bloom is quite right to say that "the usual misinterpretation of Blake's contraries" in *The Marriage* "is that they represent a simple inversion of orthodox moral categories. . . . Blake of course is doing

From *Blake and Spenser.* © 1985 by the Johns Hopkins University Press.

nothing of the kind; he is denying the orthodox categories altogether, and opposing himself both to moral 'good' and moral 'evil.' " Frye suggests that this sort of misinterpretation is due to our ignoring the fact that Blake attaches two meanings to the word *hell*, one real and the other ironic. I'm not sure that's quite satisfactory as a "guiding principle," although it will certainly help. As Bloom remarks, after quoting Frye's idea, the "voice of the Devil" is "Blake's own, but diabolical only because it will seem so to Swedenborg or any other priestly Angel." So far, so good. But when Bloom goes further to say, in plate 4 ("The voice of the Devil"), that "Blake speaks straight for once" for he "really does believe that Energy is the only life, and is from the body," are we meant to understand *these* words of the devil (for they are the devil's words) as Blakean gospel, *despite* our being "priestly angels"? Apparently—for energy, Bloom later and rather surreptitiously translates into "energetic world of imaginings" and "creative exuberance." The transition as such is merely stated rather than examined: "sexual exuberance, breaking the bounds of restraint and entering a fullness that Angelic Reasonc considers excess, will lead to a perception of a redeemed nature, though this perception itself must seem unlawful to fallen reason."

The problem here is not that Bloom is wrong (indeed, his essay in *Blake's Apocalypse* and its predecessor in article form are, to my mind, still the best commentaries on *The Marriage*) but that there is no clear way for one immersed in Blake to know why he is wrong. And for the non-Blakean, his rightness almost becomes a matter [of] faith. This problem is at its most intense in the "Proverbs of Hell." Though "of Hell," they are not spoken by a devil but rather by a Lucianic traveler in Hell who, like a good tourist, has collected some proverbs, "thinking that as the sayings used in a nation, mark its character," so these will reveal the Nation of Hell's wisdom "better than any description of buildings or garments." In assuming that Blake here speaks *in propria persona,* Bloom establishes a quadripartite structure for the proverbs as a whole, based on his assumption that they "exist to break down orthodox categories of thought and morality." Nevertheless, they "form overlapping groups" that are "largely defined by their imagery." The fact that the imagery "is presented in a variety of ironic disguises" does not inhibit Bloom's conveniently translating it into the four-square paradigm. Finally, we are left with this: "the Proverbs should mean a variety of things, quite correctly, to different readers." If they do, as indeed they have proved to have done, precisely how we are to identify "the laws of artistic creation" that Bloom sees Blake creating in this series of aphorisms is left unspoken. The Devil's initiatory "sentence" ("now perceived by the minds of men, & read by them on earth") with which the proverbs are launched is, we forget to note, not a statement but a question:

How do you know but ev'ry Bird that cuts the airy way,

Is an immense world of delight, clos'd by your senses five?

How indeed?

It is well known that Blake adapted these lines from Chatterton's *Bristowe Tragedie*. But, if Blake meant it "to serve as an introductory motto" to the "Proverbs of Hell," with Chatterton thus serving as "a prophet of later poets' sensibilities," the choice is an odd one. The lines are spoken by Syr Charles Bawdin, who is about to be executed; the particular context of the lines is his memory of escapes from death in battle and the consequent irony of his present predicament. The absurd irrelevance to Blake's context and apparent purposes makes one wonder what point he had in mind in making the allusion at all — if indeed the lines are more than an unconscious (or perhaps conscious) echo of a felicitous phrase. Yet such unwilled echoes or borrowings for essentially extrinsic purposes are rarely Blake's way. The trope of "cutting the air" (or water) has a venerable history in literature as far back as Homer, Virgil, and Ovid. Nevertheless, there is a distinct and recognizable allusion in Chatterton's lines — to Spenser. In book 2 of *The Faerie Queene*, overcome by his three-day ordeal in Mammon's cave, Guyon's "enfeebled spright" is "laid in swowne" and hence made vulnerable to capture and certain "execution" by Pyrochles and Cymochles. But at this critical moment, Spenser materializes for Guyon a guardian angel, among whose accouterments are

> two sharpe winged sheares
> Decked with diuerse plumes, like painted Iayes,
> [That] were fixed at his backe, to cut his ayerie ways.
> (8.5)

This miraculous intercession is preceded by Spenser's account of "care in heauen" for "creatures bace, / That may compassion of their euils moue." This care consists of "heauenly spirits" who

> with golden pineons, cleaue
> The flitting skyes, like flying Pursuiuant,
> Against foule feends to aide vs millitant.
> (8.1–2)

Guyon's particular heavenly spirit is, says Spenser,

> Like as *Cupido* on *Idaean* hill,
> When hauing laid his cruell bow away,
> And mortall arrowes, wherewith he doth fill
> The world with murdrous spoiles and bloudie pray.
> (8.6)

Chatterton, an inveterate and incorrigible literary thief, has here stolen quite marvelously, translating Spenser's Cupid simile, with its Petrarchan murder, darts of love, and bloody prey, into the visceral cruelty of Syr Charles's imprisonment and impending death—all the while alluding to the Spenserian ministrations of a heavenly spirit. We should not be surprised, then, to find Syr Charles, in the rest of the poem, reasserting the righteousness of his life and career and his readiness to die in the knowledge that a future life awaits him in "the land of bliss" with "God in Heaven."

The Devil's question in *The Marriage,* then, is at least in some measure answered by the Chatterton-Spenser allusion (there is no doubt, I think, that Blake knew both passages): we know that every bird that cuts the airy way is an immense world of delight because of "th' exceeding grace / Of highest God" who sends such "blessed Angels . . . to and fro" (8.1). But something is still awry; grace of this kind is hardly a Blakean tenet, and even if it were, the love of God that inspires such grace hardly seems appropriate to the "Proverbs of Hell." In *An Hymne of Heauenlie Love,* however, the nine orders of angels are equipped "with nimble wings to cut the skies, / When he [God] them on his messages doth send" (66–67), a passage that may very well have suggested to Blake an appropriate conversion of angel-messengers into a Devil who delivers his message to "the minds of men" "with corroding fires."

Despite the attractiveness of the Spenser-Chatterton connection to Blake's "introduction," it does not exhaust Blake's remarkable pattern of allusion. Milton's Satan and his hosts are habitually cloud-enwrapped, but in *Paradise Regained* "the Adversary" summons "all his mighty Peers, / Within thick clouds and dark ten-fold involv'd" (1.38–41), and the Deluge is presaged by clouds "with black wings / Wide hovering" (11.738–39). In *Paradise Lost* Beelzebub's advice to the fallen angels is not "to sit in darkness here / Hatching vain empires" but rather, in Milton's own words, "earth with hell / To mingle and involve" (2.377–78, 383–84); he then calls for a champion to

> tempt with wand'ring feet
> The dark unbottomed infinite abyss
> And though the palpable obscure find out
> His uncouth way, or spread his airy flight
> Upborne with indefatigable wings
> Over the vast abrupt, ere he arrive
> The happy isle.
>
> (2.404–10)

Later in his confrontation with Sin and Death, Satan announces his mission of treading

Th' unfounded deep, and through the void immense
To search with wand'ring quest a place foretold.
. . . . . . . . . . . . . . . . . . . . . . . . .
Created vast and round, a place of bliss.

(2.829–33)

"Into this wild abyss, / The Womb of Nature and perhaps her grave," "the wary Fiend" stands "on the brink of hell and looked a while" (2.910–11, 917–18), just as earlier "those bad angels" were "Hovering on wing under the cope of hell / 'Twixt upper, nether, and surrounding fires" (1.345–46).

Here then are both Blake's "abyss of the five senses" (Milton's Hell and Chaos) and his "present world," his Devil-Satan about to discover the "immense world of delight" (see 5.88) that is the unfallen Eden, where "Nature's whole wealth" is "To all delight of human sense exposed" (4.206), a world that he will corrupt by means of the abyss's very senses that are "delighted." Furthermore, the "immense world of delight" also seems to be Beelzebub's vision of the fallen angels' possible reentry into heaven, their escape from "corroding fires":

or else in some mild zone
Dwell not unvisited of heav'n's fair light
Secure, and at the bright'ning orient beam
Purge off this gloom; the soft delicious air
To heal the scar of these corrosive fires
Shall breathe her balm.

(2.397–402)

The permutations are dazzling, for Blake at once celebrates and condemns Milton's fallen host and leader, as if to warn us not to take his diabolical gospel (and its book of proverbs) uncritically or unilaterally. Satan's energy may be impressive, but he is also a destructive manipulator of the senses; however prolific (in Blake's sense of that term in *The Marriage*), he is as much a devourer as the maw of his progeny, Sin and Death. Furthermore, the immense world of delight which he suggests is somehow "in" every bird that cuts the airy way (as distinct from Blake's more famous "World in a Grain of Sand,") is equally ambiguous; it is Milton's Eden, but it may also be Blake's (they are obviously not the same). And finally, while Blake's Devil employs his corrosives creatively to etch the plates that will be perceived by the minds of men, Milton's devils seek an immense world of delight that is both free of "corrosive fires" and mild and balmy to the senses.

If we return now to the Proverb of Hell with which we started, several corrosive "sentences" may now be perceived by our minds. For Milton, the road of sensory excess clearly does not lead to the palace of wisdom, though that is precisely the bottom line of Satan's temptation of Eve. To her, the fruit of the forbidden tree is itself "excess" (9.648), and, once fallen, she and Adam are perceived by God as "Bewailing their excess" (11.111). And, of course, Eve's expression of gratitude to the most "precious of all trees / In Paradise" includes its opening for her of "wisdom's way" (9.798, 809). But to assume from this that Blake, pursuing his already announced dissatisfaction with *Paradise Lost* earlier in *The Marriage*, therefore does believe that the road of excess leads to the palace of wisdom is to attribute to him the same error of either/or that so infuriates him in Milton's conception. One should be reminded here that, as Milton says earlier, in another context of excess,

> neither man nor angel can discern
> Hypocrisy, the only evil that walks
> Invisible, except to God alone,
> By his permissive will, through heav'n and earth;
> And oft though wisdom wake, suspicion sleeps
> At wisdom's gate, and to simplicity
> Resigns her charge, while goodness thinks no ill
> Where no ill seems.
>
> (3.682–91)

Thus, even Uriel, the "sharpest-sighted Spirit of all in heav'n," is beguiled by Satan's desire to know God's full creation so that he may praise "The Universal Maker." Uriel's response to Satan is directly apropos Blake's proverb:

> "Fair Angel, thy desire which tends to know
> The works of God, thereby to glorify
> The great Work-master, leads to no excess
> That reaches blame, but rather merits praise
> The more it seems excess. . . ."
>
> (3.691, 676, 694–98)

The critical points to be adduced from all of this with respect to the authoritativeness of any "sentence" in *The Marriage of Heaven and Hell* are at least two: (1) Milton's Satan, and hence Blake's Devil, is not always "right" nor are angels always wrong; and (2), most important, the authority of rightness resides more often than not in our perception and understanding of the nature of Blake's allusions. Another way to state the first of these is to say that all "conventional wisdom" in *The Marriage* is not to be merely turned upside down or inside out to arrive at Blakean "truth" (the point that Bloom makes); and another way to state the second is to say that whatever Blake ricochets off of the conventionalities of Spenserian or Miltonic (and, we should add, biblical) texts is to be taken as the "real" truth. Thus, as plate 5 of *The Marriage* imperiously declaims, in *Paradise Lost* Messiah is "Reason" and "the original Archangel or possessor of the command of the heavenly host, is calld the Devil or Satan." Hence according to "The Devils account," it is "Messiah" who "fell. & formed a heaven of what he stole from the Abyss"—that is to say, put bluntly, Milton's cosmic geography is upside down. Now in one sense, this may indeed be "surpassingly excellent [literary] analysis," as Bloom says, but in another it is arrant nonsense. And, more to the point, Blake knows it is nonsense, as the ridiculously pedantic "Note" at the end of the passage, with its wry political metaphor, suggests. "Parties" have nothing to do with the matter. If Milton were of the Angels' party, he would be Swedenborg and *Paradise Lost* would be just another spiritual travelogue. That the poem as we have it is, in Blake's view, redeemable argues Milton's confusion, not a fundamental error. The negations of nonpoetry (unpoetry) are not redeemable, as Swedenborg is not; the eternal contraries are. "Error can never be redeemd in all Eternity." Man, and poets, can only be redeemed from "Errors Power," *from* Satan who, *in propria persona*, "fall'n from his station . . . never can be redeem'd" (*Milton* 11.22).

In some sense, then, we are called upon in *The Marriage* to redeem the diabolical Blake from the excesses of his own apparent "correctives" to Swedenborgian, angelic, Spenserian, Miltonic "error"—which we can do not by simply reading in an infernal sense but by perceiving with our whole minds. Hell may be, as Frye says, "this world as it appears to the repressed imagination" (angels), but it is equally true that this world is "heaven" only in the eyes of devils, the unrepressed imagination. In fact, *this* world is neither—nor, more importantly, is it merely a "balance" between the two. "Balance," as Eaves correctly argues, "avoids both extremes of imbalance," a kind of *via media* or *discordia concors* that is, to Blake, but a benighted accommodation to an erroneous perception. "Wholeness," Eaves goes on, "is itself an extreme, its opposite being 'fragmentation.' " Bloom seems to me as wrong as the advocates of such a Blakean accommodation when he argues that the reader must "move constantly from a defiant celebration of heretofore repressed energies to a realization that the freed energies must accept a bounding outline, a lessened but still existent world of confining mental forms." If Reason, as *The Marriage* tells us, "is the bound or outward circumference of Energy," then Energy must be the center that is mentally confined. However, if Energy is the bound or outward circumference of Reason, the geometric metaphor remains just as geometric—no matter who or what does the confining. One metaphysic is no less tyrannical than another. For Blake, Dryden is a perfect instance of this in his attempt to "finish" *Paradise Lost* and thus to put it right, only to "degrade" Milton. If the Devil's sentence in *The Marriage,* then, is now "read by [men] on earth," Blake clearly hopes that such readers will read with their whole "intellect," which, as Shelley also knew, is both center and circumference. Only in that way may we emulate the prophetic Los, who "reads the Stars of Albion" while his rational spectre "reads the Voids / Between the Stars" (*Jerusalem* 91.36–37). The latter is "the Newtonian who reads Not & cannot Read" because he "is oppressed by his own Reasonings & Experiments" (letter to Richard Phillips).

In the same letter from which this last phrase is taken, Blake concludes with uncharacteristic humility, "We are all subject to Error." Yes—but the road of excess is not, thereby, the way to infallibility, for Blake or for Adam and Eve. It is rather (as I now revive Spenser from the limbo of this prolegomenon) the way to, among other places, the Bower of Bliss. Blake, of course, did not need to open his Spenser to discover the age-old ideas of temperance, moderation, and the golden mean. In *Milton,* for example, he cites the familiar classical quaternion of "Temperance, Prudence, Justice, Fortitude" as "the four pillars of Tyranny" (29[31].49). And there is no specific "Bower of Bliss" in his works. Nevertheless, it is difficult to imagine his being indifferent to the central principles (and principals) of book 2 of *The Faerie Queene,* which I believe stuck in his memory (and in his craw) as vividly as the equally widespread and commonplace Petrarchisms of the *Amoretti.*

What seems striking at first glance to the student of Blake, as Guyon and the Palmer enter upon the road to the bower, are the apparently minor roles Spenser assigns to both Excesse and Genius, both of whose allegorical names might well be straight out of Blake. Blake's idea of Genius, of course, underlies virtually all his thought, most centrally that "the Poetic Genius" is "the true Man," and "that the body or outward form of Man is derived from the Poetic Genius. Likewise that the forms of all things are derived from their Genius. which by the Ancients was call'd an Angel & Spirit & Demon" (*All Religions Are One*). Thus, it is not that "energies" ("the Poetic Genius") "accept" a confining form but rather that energies exfoliate into the "forms of all things," including man. But the "form" of man is his soul-body, the Human form divine rather than the human abstract. Only to be the fallen does it appear that Reason is the bound or outward circumference of energy.

Spenser's version of this is defined in book 2 as a "contrary" to the false Genius at Acrasia's gate, who is "quite contrary" to

> that celestiall powre, to whom the care
> Of life, and generation of all
> That liues, pertaines in charge particulare,
> Who wondrous things concerning our welfare,
> And straunge phantomes doth let vs oft foresee,

And oft of secret ill bids vs beware:
That is our Selfe, whom though we do not see,
Yet each doth in him selfe it well perceiue to bee.

(7.47)

This "true" Genius, Agdistes, Spenser assigns to the Garden of Adonis, and he is "a God" as "sage Antiquity / Did wisely make" him (12.48). What is missing from Spenser's conception of the essential self "we do not see" but know is there is Blake's qualifying adjective, the idea of the Imagination in every man as his true self (as Milton's true self is Milton as "true Poet"). It is possible, however, that Blake built this idea at least in part upon Spenser's notion of "that celestiall powre" which "straunge phantomes doth let vs oft foresee," although he certainly would not have been pleased by Spenser's choice of words. At the same time, the Genius of the Garden of Adonis could not have satisfied him at all as the ushering agent into an endless cycle of birth, life, decay, and death.

Even more ominously, though, Acrasia's Genius is an agent of illusion, a "foe of life, that good enuyes to all," and, most importantly, who "secretly doth vs procure to fall, / Through guilefull semblaunts, which he makes vs see." Blake would not have missed the echoes of this guilefulness in Milton's Satan (not to mention Archimago and Duessa), and the nature of this connection ought to give us pause when our minds rush to embrace as "Blakean" the excesses of Satan as desiderata. Spenser's Excesse is a similarly ambiguous figure. Although minor in the sense of her brief role in canto xii, she is in many ways the presiding allegorical power of the entire book, manifest in Mordant, Perissa and Elissa, Furor and Occasion, Pyrochles and Cymochles, Phaedria, Mammon, and Maleger, as well as a number of lesser figures and allegorical landscapes and loci. Her ambiguity (for Blake) inheres in the fact that, although she stands in firm opposition to the prudence and temperance of Guyon and the Palmer (both these virtues, we recall from *Milton*, among the pillars of tyranny), subscribing to her creed leads not only to the animalistic excesses of Maleger's troops assailing Alma's castle but also to the "lewd loues, and wastfull luxuree" in which Acrasia's "lovers" spend their days, goods, and bodies in sterile and "horrible enchantment" (2.12.80). The fundamental horror is the transformation of man into beast—for Blake, the defacing of the human form divine into the "donghill kind" represented by Grille (the same transformation, of course, that Blake knew in the Circe myth but also, closer to his heart and mind, in *Comus*—and, retransformed, in his own poems, "The Human Abstract" and "A Divine Image".

For Spenser and Milton this situation involves no dilemma: temperance and/or chastity and / or prudence and / or moderation—as well as, even more fundamentally, the reasonable mind that gives birth to and sustains those virtues—solve all such apparent problems. Spenser's Medina is one of the classic instances of the establishment and maintenance of the golden mean; her two sisters, Perissa and Elissa, are the too-much and too-little extremes. Of these, the "excessive" Perissa had

> No measure in her mood, no rule of right,
> But poured out in pleasure and delight;
> In wine and meats she flowd aboue the bancke,
> And in excess exceeded her owne might.
>
> (2.2.36)

Her suitor is properly Sans-loy. Milton's version of this is inherent in *Comus*, but he articulates the principle more precisely in Spenser's terms (as well as Aristotle's and Seneca's before him) in book 11 of *Paradise Lost.* There Michael tells the fallen Adam:

> "There is . . . if thou well observe
> The rule of *Not too much,* by temperance taught
> In what thou eat'st and drink'st, seeking from thence
> Due Nourishment, not gluttonous delight."
>
> (530–33)

Michael's maxim is immediately followed by "another sight" that he conjures up to Adam (one to which I alluded in the previous chapter), the "bevy of fair women, richly gay," who sashay into the sight of the apparently "just men." "In gems and wanton dress" they were and

> to the harp they sung
> Soft amorous ditties, and in dance came on:
> The men, though grave, eyed them, and let their eyes
> Rove without rein, till in the amorous net
> Fast caught, they liked, and each his liking chose.
>
> (577, 582–87)

Adam mistakes this vision for a portent of "peaceful days" wherein "Nature seems fulfilled in all her ends" (600–602), and Michael abruptly corrects his judgment:

> Those tents thou saw'st so pleasant, were the tents
> Of wickedness

and

> that fair female troop thou saw'st, that seemed
> Of goddesses, so blithe, so smooth, so gay,

are "empty of all good,"

> Bred only and completed to the taste
> Of lustful appetence, to sing, to dance,
> To dress, and troll the tongue, and roll the eye,

the result of all of this being the just men's yielding up of "all their virtue" and swimming in excess of "joy." And, Michael adds in language Blake clearly borrowed for one of his Proverbs of Hell, for this excessive joy "The world erelong a world of tears must weep" (607–8, 614–16, 618–20, 623, 627). Blake's version is "Excess of sorrow laughs. Excess of joy weeps," just as his version of Michael's initial maxim is the coda of the Proverbs of Hell: "Enough! or Too much" (or, the earlier proverb: "You never know what is enough unless you know what is more than enough").

In this last proverb, the mental battle between Blake and his two predecessors seems to me joined, and our final understanding of the "wisdom" of Blake's apparently sanctioned "road of excess" inheres in our previous understanding of what he means by "enough." "Reason," in the sense employed by Spenser and Milton (and in both classical and Christian traditions), is clearly anathema. For Blake *that* reason is fallen Urizen, whose iron decalogue consists of

> One command, one joy, one desire,
> One curse, one weight, one measure
> One King, one God, one Law.
>
> (Book of Urizen)

The vertical symmetry here is striking: command-curse-King, joy-weight-God, desire-measure-Law—each quite literally undermining the triplets just above:

> peace, . . . love, . . . unity:
> . . . pity, compassion, forgiveness.

The equable oneness of "the human form divine," announced so stirringly in "The Divine Image," here becomes the one law of the one self-appointed god and king, reigning (and warring) under the banner of reason. At the other end of the scale, "too much," or (in Milton's words) "more than enough," is established, as it were, for both Milton and Spenser by God through Nature only so "that temperance may be tried" (*Paradise Lost*, 11, 805).

The "doctrine of enough" is far from explicit or even clear in Blake, his discussion of it limited entirely to the passages in *The Marriage* I have cited; except for a handful of conventional poetic usages, he seems to reserve the word for equally conventional use in his prose. We must, then, look elsewhere to get to the center of the question of "Enough! or Too much" and the analogous problem of the true relationship between "excess" and "wisdom." Bloom (and others) explains away the problem by relegating the terms to an "antinomian rhetoric" whose "shock value" is geared "to clarify the role of the contraries." While that is difficult to disagree with, I do not believe that it is the whole story. Closer to the whole story is Bloom's *en passant* remark with which I have already taken issue: "Blake asks . . . his reader . . . to move constantly from a defiant celebration of heretofore repressed energies to a realization that the freed energies must accept a bounding outline, a lessened but still existent world of confining mental forms." To make the sentence mean what I think Bloom intends it to mean (or what I would like to think it means) necessitates a clearer understanding of Urizen. "Reason *and* Energy," *The Marriage* announces clearly, "are necessary to *Human* existence" (my italics). Furthermore, "Energy . . . is alone from the Body" and "Reason . . . is alone from the Soul." So far, so good. But then we are told that "Man has no Body distinct from his Soul," hence no Energy "distinct" from Reason. What is "calld" Body-Energy "is a portion of" Soul-Reason "discerned by the five Senses, the chief inlets of Soul in this age." The labeling or naming of body as "Body" (and energy as "Energy"), then, is a product of sensory perception plus reason, an "idea" in Locke's sense of that word. But "inlets" is a curious word here. In *Europe* the senses are *outlets:*

> thro' one he breathes the air;
> Thro' one, hears music of the spheres; thro' one, the eternal vine
> Flourishes, that he may recieve the grapes; thro' one can look.
> And see small portions of the eternal world that ever groweth;
> Thro' one, himself pass out what time he please, but we will not.

That seems clear, but if we change the senses to inlets and especially "inlets of Soul," we are (or Blake is) in the peculiar position of saying that, through the senses, "portions" of soul (and therefore portions of reason) infiltrate the body; or, given the ambiguousness of the prepositional construction, the Soul's-Reason's capacity to perceive (receive) "reality" is severely limited by the age's reduced perceptual capacities—in the language of the *Europe* passage just alluded to, by having "infinite Window" reduced to "five windows."

The Devil's conclusion to this crucial section of *The Marriage* thus emerges in its ambiguous confutation as Blake's "correction" of the Devil's one-sided diabolism: Energy may be the only life and is from the body, and Reason is the bound or outward circumference of Energy, but we already know from the preceding "principle" that "Man has no Body distinct from his Soul." Thus, if Reason is the bound or outward circumference of energy, the traditional conception of the soul within the prison of the body is turned inside out; the soul

(Reason) is now the sheath or envelope within which Body-Energy resides, and its perceptual and experiential *outlets* are the five senses of *Europe*. Blake's quarrel with Spenser and Milton, then, is not merely over their separation of body and soul but over their myopic inversion of the nature of that separation—which is to say their erroneous and pernicious "calling" of the "real" body "Soul," and the "real" soul "Body." The *Blakean* truth of "the road of excess" proverb is, then, the seemingly curious but meticulously prepared-for proverb that his speaker could not find in Hell: the road of sensory excess leads to the soul's "enough," which is the "All" that "satisfies" Man (*There Is No Natural Religion*). Or, to return to Blake's own terminology, "Energy is *Eternal* Delight" (my italics) because Energy is not distinct from Reason but only that portion *of* Reason "discernd by the five Senses." In this world, *mere* energy (the excesses of the body) leads only to bowers of bliss, Comus's orgies, Eve's fall, and, in Blake's prophetic terms, the sensual agonies and perversion of Vala's world. And *mere* reason leads but to the endless destruction of bowers of bliss. Analogously, Urizen's world (*fallen* Reason, the fallen soul) is "the outward circumference" (in the language of *The Marriage*) of that of Vala (the body of Nature); yet, at the same time, his world *is* hers and he is "Stung with the odours of Nature" as he explores "his dens around" and uncreates the world in good Genesis (and Miltonic and Spenserian) fashion:

> He form'd a line & a plummet
> To divide the Abyss beneath.
> He form'd a dividing rule:
>
> He formed scales to weigh;
> He formed massy weights;
> He formed a brazen quadrant;
> He formed golden compasses
> And began to explore the Abyss
> And he planted a garden of fruits
> (*Book of Urizen*, 20.31–41)

—right in the middle of *Paradise Lost* and the Garden of Adonis. And, like Milton's and Spenser's God,

> he saw
> That no flesh *nor spirit* could keep
> His iron laws one moment.
> (23.25–26; my italics)

"For he saw that life liv'd on death" (23.27) necessitating the spinning, weaving, and knotting of "The Net of Religion" *in* "the human brain" (24.21–22). In turn, the human brain (that is to say, the fallen soul)

> form'd laws of prudence, and call'd them
> The eternal laws of God

> (28.6–7)

—yet another naming rationally to circumference an "idea."

It is a stunning history. But for my purposes here, we must not lose sight of its origins in *The Marriage* and its contraries. Spenser's and Milton's problem was not that they did not recognize the eternal contraries as "necessary to Human existence," but rather that they had them backward. The antinomian rhetoric of *The Marriage,* then, is in part calculated to reverse that fundamental error. At the same time, however, that same rhetoric, "read" by imaginative minds (not that of Devils *or* Angels), is calculated to reveal the eternal oneness of the contraries that, in the fallen world ("Human existence"), are torn asunder— thus making them merely "necessary." "Hell is the outward or external of heaven," Blake wrote as early as his annotations to Swedenborg's *Heaven and Hell,* but even more crucially, hell "is of the body of the lord. for nothing is destroyd." And, succinctly, "Heaven and Hell are born together" (annotations to Swedenborg's *Divine Love and Divine Wisdom*).

To put the matter in terms of perception, an infinite sense perception is imaginative perception. Thus on plate 12 of *The Marriage,* Isaiah can say in apparent contradiction, "I saw no God. nor heard any, in a finite organical perception; but my senses [that is, my infinite "organical perception"] discover'd the infinite in every thing." Similarly, "The ancient Poets" (Blake's "Poetic Genius" who "is the true Man") perceived *their* world with "enlarged & numerous senses." In one sense, this means that such men contain their worlds precisely as the four redeemed zoas (senses) *are* the Eternity (at the apocalyptic close of *Jerusalem*) in which they walk "To & fro . . . as One Man reflecting each in each & clearly seen / And seeing." They are both the center, from which they drive "outward the Body of Death in an Eternal Death & Resurrection," and "the Outline the Circumference & Form, for ever." More simply, the eternal senses redeemed are the Imagination; Urizen redeemed is Imagination (Reason, not reason); the body redeemed is Imagination (soul); hell redeemed is Imagination (heaven); and so on. If "Heaven & Hell are born together," their subsequent "marriage" is possible only if they are perceived to be born apart. Thus in plate 3 of *The Marriage* "a *new* heaven is begun," but it is only thirty-three years later that (presumably) the old "Eternal Hell revives" (my italics.) Under all its antinomian rhetoric, then, as well as its diabolical "wisdom," lies the Blakean wisdom that the "world" of hell is just as illusory as the "world" of heaven. Each represents a "metaphysics" that each imposes on the other. The imaginative truth of the matter is the *eternal* state of "marriage" in which all things eternally are. Blake's anti-Swedenborgian, anti-Miltonic, anti-Spenserian, and antibiblical propaganda document is, imaginatively, not a program (or "progression") which, if followed, will lead to a marriage, but rather a continuous and repetitive reassertion and celebration of the eternality of Marriage. That is to say, it is not, nor did Blake intend it to be, anything like "The Bible of Hell" or any other kind of bible or "sacred code." It is, instead, the ultimate epithalamium for the marriage that is the composite art of *The Marriage*. It is also a glorious celebration of the resurrection, for in the eternal body of Christ, The Marriage takes place, and "none shall want her mate" for "his spirit it hath gathered them"; and "they shall possess it for ever, from generation to generation shall they dwell therein" (Isa. 34:16–17). Or, as Blake put it, citing Isaiah 34 and 35, this is "the return of Adam to Paradise" — the *eternal* paradise that "revives" (lives again, anew, still), not "the Eternal Hell."

# Chronology

1757    Born November 28 in London.

1771    Apprenticed to James Basire, an engraver.

1782    Married to Catherine Boucher.

1783    *Poetical Sketches* published, containing poems written 1769–78.

1787    Death of Robert Blake, the poet's beloved younger brother.

1789    Engraving of *Songs of Innocence* and *The Book of Thel.*

1790    Writes *The Marriage of Heaven and Hell* at the age of thirty-three.

1791    Printing of *The French Revolution* by left-wing publisher Joseph Johnson, but the poem is abandoned in proof sheets.

1793    Engraving of *America* and *Visions of the Daughters of Albion.*

1794    Engraving of *Songs of Experience, Europe,* and *The Book of Urizen.*

1795    Engraving of *The Book of Los, The Song of Los,* and *The Book of Ahania.*

1797    Begins to write *Vala,* or *The Four Zoas.*

1800    Goes with wife to Felpham, Sussex, to live and work with William Hayley.

1803    Quarrels with Hayley and returns to London.

1804    Is tried for sedition and acquitted after being accused by a soldier, John Scholfield. Blake dates *Milton* and *Jerusalem* as of this year, but they are believed to have been finished rather later.

1809    Exhibits his paintings, but sells none. *A Descriptive Catalogue,* written for the exhibition, survives, and contains his remarkable criticism of Chaucer.

1818    Becomes mentor to younger painters: John Linnell, Samuel Palmer, Edward Calvert, George Richmond.

1820    Woodcuts to Virgil's *Pastorals.*

1825    Completes engravings for the Book of Job.

1826    Completes illustrations to Dante.

1827    Dies on August 12.

# Contributors

HAROLD BLOOM, Sterling Professor of the Humanities at Yale University, is the author of *The Anxiety of Influence, Poetry and Repression,* and many other volumes of literary criticism. His forthcoming study, *Freud: Transference and Authority,* attempts a full-scale reading of all of Freud's major writings. A MacArthur Prize Fellow, he is general editor of five series of literary criticism published by Chelsea House.

NORTHROP FRYE is University Professor Emeritus at the University of Toronto. One of the principal literary theorists of our century, he is the author of *Fearful Symmetry, Anatomy of Criticism,* and *The Great Code.*

DAVID V. ERDMAN, Professor of English at the University of the State of New York at Stony Brook, is a renowned historical and textual authority on Blake. He is the editor of the definitive editions of Blake's writings and illuminated books, and the author of *Prophet against Empire.*

THOMAS R. FROSCH is Professor of English at Queens College. In addition to his book, *The Awakening of Albion,* he has published many poems and critical essays.

MARTIN K. NURMI is Professor of English at Kent State University. His books include *Blake's Marriage of Heaven and Hell* and *William Blake.*

LEOPOLD DAMROSCH, JR., is Professor of English at the University of Virginia. He is the author of *Samuel Johnson and the Tragic Sense* and *Symbol and Truth in Blake's Myth.*

DIANA HUME GEORGE teaches in the English department at Pennsylvania State University, Behrend College. She is the author of *Blake and Freud.*

STEWART CREHAN is Professor of English at the University of Zambia at Lusaka and the author of *Blake in Context.*

Robert Gleckner is Professor of English at Duke University. His books include *Byron and the Ruins of Paradise, The Piper and the Bard,* and *Blake and Spenser.* He has also written many critical essays on Blake and on Joyce.

# Bibliography

Adams, Hazard, *William Blake*. Philadelphia: Folcroft, 1963.

Bloom, Harold. *Blake's Apocalypse: A Study in Poetic Argument*. Ithaca: Cornell University Press, 1970.

Bogan, James, and Fred Goss, eds. *Sparks of Fire: Blake in a New Age*. Richmond, Calif.: North Atlantic Books, 1982.

Bronowski, Jacob. *William Blake and the Age of Revolution*. London: Routledge & Kegan Paul, 1972.

Damon, Samuel Foster. *William Blake: His Philosophy and Symbols*. Gloucester, Mass.: Peter Smith Publisher, 1978.

Damrosch, Leopold. *Symbol and Truth in Blake's Myth*. Princeton: Princeton University Press, 1980.

Deen, Leonard W. "Poetic Genius and Mental Flight." In *Conversing in Paradise: Poetic Genius and Identity-as-Community in Blake's* Los, 20–48. Columbia: University of Missouri Press, 1983.

DiSalvo, Jackie. *War of the Titans: Blake's Critique of Milton and the Politics of Religion*. Pittsburgh: University of Pittsburgh Press, 1983.

Dorfman, Deborah. *Blake in the Nineteenth Century: His Reputation as a Poet from Gilchrist to Yeats*. New Haven: Yale University Press, 1969.

Eaves, Morris. *William Blake's Theory of Art*. Princeton: Princeton University Press, 1982.

Erdman, David V. *Blake: Prophet against Empire*. Princeton: Princeton University Press, 1969.

Essick, Robert N., and Donald Pearce, eds. *Blake in His Time*. Bloomington: Indiana University Press, 1978.

Frye, Northrop. *Blake: A Collection of Critical Essays*. Englewood Cliffs, N.J.: Prentice-Hall, 1966.

————. *Fearful Symmetry: A Study of William Blake*. Princeton: Princeton University Press, 1947.

Gallant, Christine. *Blake and the Assimilation of Chaos*. Princeton: Princeton University Press, 1978.

George, Diana Hume. *Blake and Freud*. Ithaca: Cornell University Press, 1980.

Gleckner, Robert. *The Piper and the Bard: A Study of William Blake*. Detroit: Wayne State University Press, 1959.

Holstein, Michael E. "Crooked Roads without Improvement: Blake's 'Proverbs of Hell.'" *Genre* 8 (1975): 26–41.

Howard, John. *Infernal Poetics: Poetic Structures in Blake's Lambeth Prophecies.* Rutherford, N.J.: Fairleigh Dickinson University Press, 1984.

Keynes, Geoffrey, ed. *The Marriage of Heaven and Hell.* New York: Oxford University Press, 1975.

Klonsky, Milton. *William Blake: A Seer and His Visions.* New York: Harmony Books, 1977.

Mellor, Anne Kostelanetz. *Blake's Human Form Divine.* Berkeley and Los Angeles: University of California Press, 1974.

Mitchell, W. J. T. "Style as Epistemology: Blake and the Movement toward Abstraction in Romantic Art." *Studies in Romanticism* 16 (Spring 1977): 145–64.

Niimi, Hatsuko. "The Proverbial Language of Blake's *Marriage of Heaven and Hell.*" *Studies in English Literature* (Tokyo) 58 (1982): 3–20.

Nurmi, Martin K. *William Blake.* Kent: Ohio State University Press, 1976.

O'Neill, Judith, ed. *Critics on Blake.* Coral Gables, Fla.: University of Miami Press, 1970.

Paley, Morton. *Energy and Imagination: A Study of the Development of Blake's Thought.* Oxford: Clarendon Press, 1970.

Raine, Kathleen Jessie. *Blake and the New Age.* Boston: George Allen & Unwin, 1979.

————. *William Blake.* London: Thames & Hudson, 1970.

Sabri-Tabrizi, G. F. *The "Heaven" and "Hell" of William Blake.* London: Lawrence & Wishart, 1975.

Shabetai, Karen. "Blake's Perception of Evil." *DAI* 45, no. 6 (1984): 1552C.

Spector, Sheila. "Kabbalistic Sources: Blake and His Critics." *Blake:* An Illustrated Quarterly 17, no. 3 (1983–84): 84–101.

Tannenbaum, Leslie. "Blake's News from Hell: *The Marriage of Heaven and Hell* and the Lucianic Tradition." *ELH* 43 (1976): 74–99.

Wagenknecht, David. *Blake's Night: William Blake's Vision of the Pastoral.* Cambridge, Mass.: The Belknap Press of Harvard University Press, 1973.

Webster, Brenda S. *Blake's Prophetic Psychology.* Athens: University of Georgia Press, 1983.

# Acknowledgments

"Introduction" (originally entitled *"The Marriage of Heaven and Hell"*) by Harold Bloom from *Blake's Apocalypse: A Study in Poetic Argument* by Harold Bloom, © 1963 by Harold Bloom. Reprinted by permission of Doubleday and Company, Inc.

"The Thief of Fire" by Northrop Frye from *Fearful Symmetry: A Study of William Blake* by Northrop Frye, © 1947 by Princeton University Press. Reprinted by permission of Princeton University Press and Doubleday and Company, Inc.

"The Eternal Hell Revives" by David V. Erdman from *Blake: Prophet against Empire* by David V. Erdman, © 1954, 1969 by Princeton University Press. Reprinted by permission of Princeton University Press.

"The Dialectic of *The Marriage of Heaven and Hell*" by Harold Bloom from *The Ringers in the Tower* by Harold Bloom, © 1971 by the University of Chicago. Reprinted by permission of the University of Chicago Press.

"The Body of Imagination" by Thomas R. Frosch from *The Awakening of Albion* by Thomas R. Frosch, © 1974 by Cornell University. Reprinted by permission of Cornell University Press. The quotations from Blake are from *The Poetry and Prose of William Blake*, edited by David V. Erdman, published by Doubleday and Company, Inc., 1970. Reprinted by permission. The quotations of Wordsworth and Keats are from the Oxford Standard Authors editions: *The Poetical Works of Wordsworth*, edited by Thomas Hutchinson, rev. Ernest de Selincourt (London, 1964); *The Poems of John Keats*, edited by A. W. Garrod (London, 1961). Reprinted by permission.

"Polar Being" (originally entitled *"The Marriage of Heaven and Hell"*) by Martin K. Nurmi from *William Blake* by Martin K. Nurmi, © 1975 by Martin K. Nurmi. Reprinted by permission of the author and Hutchinson & Company.

"The Problem of Dualism" (originally entitled "Contraries") by Leopold Damrosch, Jr. from *Symbol and Truth in Blake's Myth* by Leopold Damrosch, © 1980 by Princeton University Press. Reprinted by permission of Princeton University Press.

"Blake and Freud" (originally entitled "Innocence and Experience") by Diana Hume George from *Blake and Freud* by Diana Hume George, © 1980 by Cornell University.

Reprinted by permission of Cornell University Press. The poems are from *The Poetry and Prose of William Blake*, edited by David B. Erdman, published by Doubleday and Company, Inc., 1970. Reprinted by permission.

"Producers and Devourers" by Stewart Crehan from *Blake in Context* by Stewart Crehan, © 1984 by Stewart Crehan. Reprinted by permission of the Humanities Press International, Inc., Atlantic Highlands, New Jersey and Gill and Macmillan.

"Roads of Excess" by Robert F. Gleckner from *Blake and Spenser* by Robert F. Gleckner, © 1985 by the Johns Hopkins University Press. Reprinted by permission of the Johns Hopkins University Press, Baltimore/London.

# Index